F.A. CUP GIANT KILLERS

First published in 1994 by
CollinsWillow
an imprint of HarperCollins*Publishers*
London

© Geoff Tibballs 1994

A CIP catalogue record for this book
is available from the British Library

ISBN 0 00 218481 8

Designed by Stuart Perry

Photographs courtesy of The Press Association

Printed and bound in Great Britain

The author would like to thank the staffs at
Nottingham City Library and the British Newspaper
Library in Colindale for assuring such a pleasant trip
down soccer's Memory Lane, and also Michael Doggart
and Tom Whiting at CollinsWillow for their
enthusiasm for this project.

F.A.CUP GIANT KILLERS

GEOFF TIBBALLS

CollinsWillow
An Imprint of HarperCollins*Publishers*

CONTENTS

★INTRODUCTION

Rather like Kennedy's assassination, I can remember exactly what I was doing that day in 1971 when little Colchester knocked mighty Leeds out of the FA Cup. I was at Kenilworth Road, Luton, watching a local derby with Watford. The only reason I was there was because my own team, Millwall, were without a game that afternoon and Grandstand probably featured a diet of gymnastics, swimming, table tennis and pro-celebrity dominoes. The match was a predictably nondescript affair, the proceedings enlivened only by the news from someone with a radio the size of Luton's main stand, that Leeds were losing 3-0 at Colchester. Such messages at football grounds often have to be taken with a pinch of salt but this one was verified. I could hardly wait for Match of the Day.

Although like most neutrals, I was delighted to see Leeds beaten, I sympathised to a certain extent. My mind went back to the early Sixties when, in quick succession, Millwall were dumped out of the Cup by Worcester City, Bath City, Kettering Town and Hereford United. The pain at school the next day would have been excruciating, had anybody mentioned it. But none of the class took a boy who followed Millwall seriously. They weren't a proper team, they said. And that was before they'd seen them play...

A year after Colchester, it was Hereford's turn. Their first goal goes down as one of the great moments in footballing history, ranking alongside Gordon Banks' save from Pele in Mexico, Geoff Hurst's 1966 World Cup clincher and Graham Taylor's address to the linesman in Holland. Yet its architect was not a highly-paid international but a humble artisan from the lower echelons of the game, a joiner who had plied his trade with the likes of Cheltenham, Newport and then Hereford. His name was Ronnie Radford, and his astonishing 40-yarder which propelled the Southern League side to FA Cup glory at the expense of First Division Newcastle has since been repeated on TV even more often than the exploits of Messrs Banks and Hurst.

Now 52, Radford remembers it as if it were yesterday. 'My main memories are of the crowd,' he says. 'They were fantastic. We used to get gates of up to 5,000 just for Southern League matches. It is a wonderful feeling, knowing that I managed to inspire a crowd of 15,000 that day. Since then, I've imagined the goal from every part of the ground, just to visualise what it must have been like for the fans.'

It is one of the quirks of the Cup that Radford was only at Hereford in the first place because of an increased workload. 'I had been full-time at Newport but when the work started coming in, I felt I couldn't turn it down, so I went back to playing part-time and joined Hereford. Playing a big club in the Cup is what every non-League player dreams of. It's the one time in your life when you can roll up your sleeves and really enjoy your day.'

Of course, soccer giant-killing is by no means confined to the FA Cup, as Berwick Rangers in the Scottish Cup, Swindon Town in the League Cup and the USA in the 1950 World Cup will point out. But it is the FA Cup which regularly pits the lowly part-timers with the fat cats – the brickies, barmen and bus drivers with the seasoned professionals. Yeovil, Walsall, Bedford, Bishop Auckland, Norwich, Peterborough, the names trip off the tongue. Their achievements represent the ultimate in fantasy football. Their stories have been passed down over the generations, via mugs of warm Bovril, the winning goal getting better with each telling. With practice, a mis-hit with two deflections can sound like goal of the month.

Giant-killing epitomises the romance of the FA Cup. The conception may not always be immaculate – not unless you count a muddy field on a January night in Altrincham as particularly sensuous – but the end result is well worth waiting for.

Geoff Tibballs

Lockwood Brothers 2
Nottingham Forest 1

11 December 1886

A part from the long-standing association with Robin Hood, Nottingham couldn't boast too many folk heroes in the late 19th century. Brian Clough wasn't even a 'young man', Torvill and Dean were years away from their first double axle and there was not even a sound from Paper Lace, the 1970s beat combo whose chart success with 'Billy Don't Be A Hero' represents the pinnacle of the city's musical achievements. But the good citizens of Nottingham were suitably proud of their two principal football teams – Nottingham Forest and Notts County – and fully expected the former to progress to the fourth round of the FA Cup at the expense of Lockwood Brothers, a Sheffield works team who were so humble that they had to use a local hotel as their changing rooms.

The tie was staged at Bramall Lane. The *Nottingham Post* reported: 'Special trains run by the Midland and Great Northern Railway Companies conveyed some hundreds of supporters of the Reds to the cutlery town, many of them wearing the colours of the club, and great enthusiasm was manifested.' Forest were without the services of Lindley, who was otherwise engaged playing for the Corinthians against Preston, but, winning the toss, kicked off with the wind in their favour at 2.35pm , full of optimism.

However, Lockwoods were not to be taken lightly. Any team which had disposed of the likes of Long Eaton Rangers and Cleethorpes Town – as they had in previous rounds – warranted respect. The works team began brightly with McLoughlin 'most prominent' but soon Forest's superior passing enabled them to gain the upper hand. Danks shot straight at the keeper in the fifth minute before making amends with 'a capital shot' which Brook could only parry to

Norman who scored from the rebound to put the visitors ahead. By now, Forest were well on top with Brook being forced to make half a dozen saves. Then, against the run of play, Winterbottom broke away and passed to Brayshaw who crossed for Sellers to head the equaliser, the Forest defence appealing in vain for offside.

Encouraged by this goal, Lockwoods began the second half in sprightly fashion and ten minutes into it, Winterbottom broke clear again, only to be denied by Osborn at the expense of a corner. Forest's respite was short-lived. Brayshaw flighted the flag-kick to perfection and Betts headed the factory men in front.

Unwin missed the chance of an equaliser but Forest's efforts generally drew scathing criticism from the *Post* correspondent. 'The Foresters played feebly against the wind and Lockwoods had decidedly the best of it until shortly before the finish. Then the Reds rallied somewhat.' Even then, it was a short-lived flourish and the game ended with Lockwoods back on the attack, Beardsley making two fine saves to keep the deficit down to one goal.

Lockwood Brothers were able to savour their finest hour for another two months before being knocked out by West Bromwich Albion. They made their last appearance in the FA Cup the following season. To crown a miserable day for Forest, their absent team-mate, Lindley, was also on the losing side, Corinthians losing 2-0 to Preston. Perhaps the players' only consolation was that they didn't have to face Brian Clough in the dressing-room afterwards.

Lockwood Brothers: Brook; Salkeld, Stringer, Brayshaw, Betts, McLoughlin, West, Winterbottom, Hudson, Cawley, Sellers.
Nottingham Forest: Beardsley; Osborn, Hancock, Norman, Ward, Pike, Unwin, Leighton, Jeffries, Danks, Fox.
Referee: Mr H.Chaplin (Derby)
Attendance: 4,000

Millwall Athletic 2
Aston Villa 1

5 March 1900

*A*round the turn of the century, Aston Villa were just about the strongest team in the land. They had completed the 'double' in 1897, won the League again in 1899 and now, in March 1900, were on course for another League and Cup triumph. But they had encountered an unexpectedly stubborn obstacle in the quarter-finals of the Cup in the shape of Millwall Athletic, a club formed 15 years previously by a group of jam factory workers and who were stuck in ninth spot in the Southern League. The first tie at Millwall's East Ferry Road ground ended in a 1-1 draw and the replay at Villa Park finished 0-0. And so a third match proved necessary, this time at Reading.

The choice of venue turned out to be significant. It so happened that Millwall's talented amateur centre-forward, J.H.Gettins, taught in Reading and was only able to obtain time off to play in this midweek match because it was staged locally. Work commitments had forced him to miss the first replay.

With many Millwall fans taking the day off to journey to Berkshire, the teams ran out to the strains of the Reading Temperance Band. The Dockers made the livelier start, pushing Villa onto the defensive. The only threat to the Millwall goal came when the ball struck referee Lewis full in the face and rebounded to a Villa forward. The danger was cleared but Mr Lewis was less fortunate and had to swap places with one of his linesmen for a few minutes.

Then Villa were dealt a double blow. On 15 minutes, Hugh Goldie's corner was spectacularly volleyed home by Herbert Banks, his rasping shot giving keeper George no chance. Four minutes later, Millwall sensationally increased their lead. Gettins, watched by his adoring pupils, lost his marker, Evans, and embarked on a mazy run which finished with a rousing shot past George.

Villa were stunned into action. From then on, they dominated proceedings but found the Millwall rearguard, in which David Smith and Arthur Millar were outstanding, in resolute mood. For their part, Millwall were reduced to breakaways, handicapped as they were by an injury to Gettins who, as the *East End News* and *London Shipping Chronicle* reported on its front page, had 'fallen lame'. Finally, nine minutes from time, Johnson found a way through the packed Millwall ranks to pull one back. Villa threw everything into attack. Garraty looked certain to equalise but Smith cleared for a corner. Then Spencer sent a long shot just wide. The *News* scribe noted: 'The Villa were making matters warm in the few remaining seconds.'

But they ran out of time. Millwall were through to the semi-final, where they lost to Southampton, while Villa, their dreams of the 'double' shattered, had to content themselves with going on to win the First Division Championship. There was much celebrating in East London that night...away from the stern gaze of the Reading Temperance Band.

Millwall: Cox; Burgess, Allen, Smith, Goldie, Millar, Dryburgh, Brearley, J.H.Gettins, Banks, Nicol.
Aston Villa: George; Spencer, Evans, Bowman, Wilkes, Noon, Athersmith, Devey, Garraty, Johnson, Templeton.
Referee: Mr Lewis
Attendance: 15,000

3

13 February 1901

*G*rand. That was the word to describe this match. 'GRAND VICTORY FOR THE KETTS' boomed the headline in the Kettering Leader although the lack of prominence given to the report, tucked away in an end column next to the cattle auction prices, suggested that if the Mayor had cut his thumb that week, it wouldn't have made it at all. It certainly was a grand result for Midland Leaguers Kettering in overcoming their supposedly superior opponents from Division Two of the Football League, away from home to boot.

The first match had ended in a 1-1 draw and for the replay at Chesterfield, the Ketts, an unimiginative nickname if ever there was one, had to call up two late replacements – Garfield, in his days before adorning Ford Capris, and Winterhalder. The latter was to prove Kettering's match winner. His selection was thus a grand decision.

'From the kick-off,' wrote the Leader, 'Chesterfield quickly invaded but Clarke was all there and cleared splendidly.' The doubts about Clarke's mental state resolved, Kettering settled down and were rewarded with an early goal, thanks to a grand piece of play from the referee. Pollock's ferocious free-kick rebounded off the hapless official straight to Webb who scored off the underside of the bar.

Chesterfield launched reprisals. Visiting skipper Draper denied Geary with a timely tackle and then blocked a shot from Munday. Baldry was then called upon to make a grand save from Thacker's drive. At the other end, McMain nearly increased Kettering's advantage but slipped at the vital moment. Not so grand.

It was the same story in the second half. Somehow Kettering held out until the 58th minute when Gooing equalised with a powerful shot from a free-kick awarded against McMain.

And so the match went into extra-time where, surprisingly, Kettering proved the stronger. McCracken had already made a grand clearance to avert one crisis before Winterhalder snatched the winner in the 104th minute, the ball brushing home defender Bell on its way into the net. Webb, just about the grandest player on view, nearly put the issue beyond doubt but 'had terribly hard lines in not scoring'. With Chesterfield unable to make further inroads, Kettering duly progressed to the second round where they were firmly put in their place to the tune of 5-0 by Middlesbrough.

And the Kettering Leader's verdict on the Chesterfield tie? 'A grandly contested game.' Quite.

Chesterfield: Hancock; McCracken, Pilgrim, Haig, Bell, Thacker, Arnold, Turner, Gooing, Munday, Geary.
Kettering Town: Baldry; Clarke, Draper, Roulston, Panter, Pollock, Webb, Garfield, McMain, Becton, Winterhalder.
Referee: Mr J.C. Tillotson (Birmingham)
Attendance: 2,000

4

New Brompton 3
Sunderland 1

11 January 1908

'From one o'clock onwards, there was a constant stream of pedestrians to the ground. Vehicles of all descriptions from the up-to-date motor-car to the coster's cart, were to be seen dashing up to the entrance and depositing their human loads.'

Chatham, Rochester and Gillingham Observer

The forerunners of Gillingham, New Brompton were enjoying an unremarkable season, occupying a berth in the lower half of the Southern League. But after defeating Shepherds Bush 6-0 in the fifth qualifying round, excitement in the Medway towns reached fever pitch when the first round draw paired them with four-times League Champions, Sunderland, the first Division One team to visit the Priestfield Road ground.

To cater for the anticipated influx of followers from Wearside, 300 loads of earth were dumped to extend the banking at the Rainham end of the ground. The New Brompton players prepared for the big match in a more leisurely manner, spending the week at Herne Bay, a coastal resort not exactly renowned for sin and debauchery.

The nights prior to the game had witnessed sharp frosts. The pitch was hard and whilst the middle was sanded, the wings were not, making the simple act of standing up a feat in itself. The Sunderland players were taking no chances and had their knees well protected in case of falls.

They certainly looked the more comfortable team during the early exchanges but Harvey and Floyd tackled soundly at the back for the underdogs. At the other end, Salter was presented with an opportunity but, to the chagrin of the *Gillingham Observer*, he 'held the leather too long and was dispossessed by Foster.' The reporter went on to compliment the Sunderland full-backs as 'a sturdy pair of defenders who kicked with rare power.'

After home keeper Martin had turned a shot from Holley on to the bar, Sunderland deservedly went ahead on 31 minutes. A McIntosh shot brought Martin to his knees with the ball lodged under him. Before he could react, the custodian was robustly charged by Holley, with the result that ball and Martin ended up in the back of the net. The referee had no hesitation in awarding a goal.

Sunderland had no time to celebrate before they were pulled back to level terms. Direct from the restart, the ball was rushed down the New Brompton right for a corner and when Hopkins' flag-kick came over, it was splendidly headed in by McGibbon. Sunderland became rattled. Ward made two further saves from McGibbon but then, in the 51st minute, Robotham hoisted the ball into the middle, Salter slipped it to McGibbon as he was about to be tackled and McGibbon ran on a few strides and drove powerfully into the corner of the net. 'Hats and sticks were wildly flung into the air.'

Tait came close to an equaliser before New Brompton settled the issue. Smith broke clear, drew Bonthron and passed to McGibbon who completed a memorable hat-trick. 'The crowd went nearly mad,' related the *Gillingham Observer*, obviously aware that they had mercifully stopped short of outright insanity.

And so New Brompton recorded a remarkable victory. They went out in the next round, after a replay to Manchester City, and it was back to basics the following season when they were unceremoniously booted out of the competition by Hastings United. Their day of glory was over. Even as Gillingham (whose name they adopted in 1912), they would never again defeat a First Division side in the FA Cup.

New Brompton: Martin; Harvey, Floyd, Lloyd, Mavin, Robotham, Hopkins, Salter, McGibbon, Hartley, Smith.
Sunderland: Ward; Bonthron, Foster, Tait, Low, Jarvie, Hogg, McIntosh, Raybould, Holley, Bridgett.
Referee: Mr W.Gilgryst (Manchester)
Attendance: 12,000

5

20 January 1908

A lthough not quite the force of the 'Old Invincibles', the Preston team of 1908 was good enough to occupy a position of respectability in the middle of the First Division. When paired with Brighton in the first round of the FA Cup that year, they were certainly expected to progress at the expense of the Sussex team who, with a mere six wins from 20 matches, found themselves at the wrong end of the Southern League table. But, like Aston Villa and Sunderland before them, Preston were in for a rude awakening from Southern League upstarts.

The teams first met on 11 January in Brighton where an equaliser just four minutes from time earned Preston a replay. That took place five days later at Deepdale and again Brighton were cheated when failing light forced the referee to abandon the game with them leading 2-1 and only eight minutes of extra time remaining.

So to a third meeting at Stamford Bridge on Monday the 20th. Brighton had enjoyed the better preparations, their Southern League fixture with Southampton on the Saturday having been abandoned after nine minutes through fog while Preston slogged out a tough match with Sunderland. After a cautious start, in which Joynes wasted an opportunity for Brighton, Preston began to take command but their forwards encountered two veritable rocks in Archer and Turner. Preston's best effort during this spell was a free-kick from Danson which flew narrowly wide. Slowly, Brighton once again gained the measure of their illustrious opponents. Hall went close with a header and then a cross by Anthony presented Joynes with an excellent chance but he nodded over when well placed.

In the 33rd minute, Brighton broke the deadlock. A long ball from Archer was flicked on by Hall for Wombwell to run on and score with a vicious shot into the roof of the net. Keeper McBride threw the ball out as it dropped, but the referee was not taken in by this piece of gamesmanship and awarded a goal. The left-wing pair of Danson and Dawson tried to spur Preston into life in the second period but Brighton soon resumed control and, in the words of the *Sussex Daily News*, 'a dashing combined run ended in Wombwell sending in a rasping drive just past the far post.' Preston tried another late rally, a Lyon free-kick flashing inches off target, but it proved third time lucky for Albion who hung on to reach the second round for the first time in their history. The *Daily Express* recounted: 'There was a wild scene of exhilaration at the close of the game in which fireworks played no inconsiderable part.' However before Cup fever could reach epidemic proportions on the South Coast, Brighton made their exit from the competition, beaten 3-0 in a second round replay by Liverpool.

Brighton & Hove Albion: Macdonald; Archer, Turner, Kent, Morris, McDonals, Joynes, Burnett, Hall, Wombwell, Anthony.
Preston North End: McBride; Lockett, Rodway, McLean, Stringfellow, Lyon, Bond, Wilson, Gillibrand, Danson, Dawson.
Referee: Mr J.H. Wilson
Attendance: 25,000

'Brighton's triumph was one gained essentially on their merits and the crowd cheered itself hoarse when the final whistle left no question that the South had vanquished the North.'

Sussex Daily News

6

14 January 1911

*I*t has been said that the sights of Crewe begin and end with the railway station, a train-spotters' paradise that acts like a magnet to anorak wearers of the northern hemisphere. The town's association with the railways was equally strong in the early years of the century but relations became strained when lowly Birmingham & District Leaguers Crewe Alexandra were drawn away to First Division Bristol City in the first round of the Cup. The Great Western Railway Company flatly refused to operate reduced fares for supporters wishing to travel to Bristol and so, in a mighty snub, the Crewe team, officials and many fans journeyed instead via Birmingham on the Midland line, these being the days of free choice, before every ticket came complete with a three page list of travel restrictions.

Those who made the trip did so with hope rather than confidence. In truth, nobody, least of all Bristol City, gave Crewe a chance. Most impartial Bristolians preferred to watch Rovers' home game with Hull which took place on the same afternoon.

It soon became apparent that City's over-confidence was to be their downfall. The *Crewe Chronicle* reported enthusiastically: 'The City began to press and Crewe likewise put on extra vigour, as the sphere travelled rapidly from end to end.' Walley had an early chance but was slow to react and Davies saw an effort ruled out for offside. Crewe's pressure was rewarded on the half-hour when Chapple, Walley and King combined for King to score with a fine ground shot.

The visitors kept up the good work after the break and 'a number of rattling good shots were sent to Bailiff for disposal.' The home keeper did well to turn a shot from King around the post but was eventually beaten again, this time by a mis-hit from Mason. By now, City, who had been unable to test Coventry in the Crewe goal since the opening minutes, were a sorry rabble and it came as no surprise when Chapple headed a third from an 80th minute corner. The Crewe supporters who had risked the wrath of the Great Western undoubtedly enjoyed their rail journey home.

Bristol City: Bailiff; Young, Cottle, Mason, Wedlock, Hankin, Clare, Gadsby, Owers, Burton, Shearman.
Crewe Alexandra: Coventry; Fletcher, Spittle, Peters, Haywood, Stanley, Mason, Davies, King, Chapple, Walley.
Referee: Mr Archer
Attendance: 8,000

'The team played a brilliant game and fully deserved the victory. Every man did his utmost and, what was more encouraging, was the fact that individualists were left in the background and there was more combination in evidence.'

Crewe captain Spittle

Cardiff City 2
Oldham Athletic 0

10 January 1920

*U*nlike Bristol City, First Division Oldham were determined not to make the mistake of underestimating their opponents when the first round draw took them to Southern League Cardiff City. 'Arthurian' in the South Wales Echo wrote that Oldham had gone to the trouble of arriving in Wales on the Tuesday before the game, adding: 'The directorate propose making Penarth their headquarters for the week, and naturally the hope is held by them that the team will be thoroughly acclimatised by Saturday.'

Obviously, Oldham felt that it would take some time to adjust to the heat, altitude and rarified air of Cardiff. As it transpired, Oldham would have been better off staying at home since they were swept aside by a rampant Cardiff side who coped magnificently with the greasy ball and soggy pitch. The *Western Mail* eulogised: 'The Cardiff City eleven played the game of their career. Not for them the kick-to-touch-at-every-available-opportunity game.' Perhaps the correspondent was getting a shade confused with rugby…

Apart from an early scare when Smith's failure to trap a cross presented Burrows with a chance which he failed to accept, it was all Cardiff. While Kneeshaw in the home goal had only one save to make in the entire match, Matthews at the other end was performing heroics to keep his side on level terms. Before half-time, he saved well from Beare, Cox and Smith and continued his one-man show in the second period. Just as Cardiff were wondering whether they would ever make the breakthrough, it came with a quarter of an hour remaining. Matthews splendidly turned a West shot aside for a corner but from the flag-kick, there was an almighty scramble which culminated in West heading home. Seven minutes later, it was all over. West sent a long ball over to Evans who worked himself into a shooting position. Evans's first effort struck a defender, but he latched on to the rebound and sent a rising shot into the net off the underside of the bar.

The success marked a turning point in Cardiff's history. The following season, they were admitted to the expanded Football League and progressed to the semi-finals of the Cup. In 1925 and 1927, they reached Wembley itself, winning the trophy on the latter occasion at the expense of Arsenal, the only time the Cup has been taken outside England.

'But for a magnificent display of goalkeeping by Matthews, the Oldham citadel would inevitably have capitulated on at least six occasions.'

Western Mail

8

Sheffield Wednesday 0
Darlington 2

19 January 1920

*T*he city of Sheffield had always been dear to the hearts of Darlington Football Club. Back in 1911 the North-Eastern Leaguers had gained a famous FA Cup victory at Sheffield United and now, nine years on, history had a chance to repeat itself at neighbours Wednesday. The omens were good for another giant-killing.

Darlington had held their own in the first tie which ended in a goalless draw and Wednesday, despite a 1-0 victory over Everton on the Saturday before the replay, were firmly rooted to the foot of the First Division. They also had a number of injury worries. It is worth noting that while Wednesday were taking on the men from Goodison, Darlington were overcoming less exalted opposition, Shildon, in the Durham Senior Cup.

Having seen nothing to frighten them at Feethams, Darlington were confident of beating Wednesday at the second attempt. Some 3,000 Darlington fans made the journey to Sheffield and were rewarded with a result which shook the football world.

Darlington, who had trained at Hillsborough on the morning of the match to get the feel of the place, were forced onto the defensive for much of the first half but Wednesday were woefully lacking in attacking ideas. And when they did threaten, Taylor marshalled the visitors' rearguard superbly. Then, after 40 minutes, Darlington centre-forward Healey strode through the middle, forcing keeper Birch to concede a corner. Winship's kick led to a scramble from which Malcolm netted, the goal being greeted with bugle calls from the jubilant Darlington fans.

Darlington never looked back. They were comfortably the more accomplished side in the second half and were always quicker to the ball as Wednesday's resolve drained away. Dickson went close before, midway through the half, McSkimming, who had a wretched game, lost the ball to Malcolm. It ran loose and developed into a race between Stevens and Blair. It was Stevens who got there first to put Darlington two up and through to the second round. There they lost 4-0 at Birmingham but had the satisfaction of being elected to the Football League in 1921. Wednesday, meanwhile, were duly relegated, finishing with a meagre 28 goals from 42 League games.

Sheffield Wednesday: Birch; McSkimming, Blair, Brittleton, Reed, Campbell, Capper, Binney, Brentnall, Mackay, Gill.
Darlington: Greig; Golightly, Taylor, Dickson, Sutcliffe, Malcolm, Kirsopp, Lawrence, Healey, Stevens, Winship.
Attendance: 52,810

'I'm proud of the boys. It was a victory after my own heart. Stamina did it.'

Darlington manager, Jack English

9

Corinthians 1
Blackburn Rovers 0

12 January 1924

The Corinthians occupied a unique position in the English game. Formed in 1882, they were strictly amateur, composed mainly of former public schoolboys and University men. They refused to take part in competitive matches until 1923 when they entered the FA Cup, and the following year sprang a major surprise when defeating First Division Blackburn Rovers in a first-round tie at Crystal Palace.

The Blackburn of 1924 may not have had the benefit of Jack Walker's millions but they were good enough to finish eighth in the League that season. But on that January afternoon, they were utterly baffled by the amateurs' unconventional tactics. Whereas the professional game favoured leaving the centre-forward alone upfield in the hope of snatching a goal, Corinthians preferred to attack through the middle en masse, in a five-man line. So, kicking into the wind in the first half, Blackburn found themselves facing a tidal wave of Corinthians' forwards. *The Times* compared Blackburn's inability to cope with these unusual tactics thus: 'A boy who can treat the first three books of Euclid with contempt is often absolutely hopeless when given a simple rider to work out for himself.' Eat your heart out, Stuart Hall.

The game set off at a tremendous pace and Corinthians' early pressure was rewarded with what turned out to be the decisive goal after 15 minutes. K.E.Hegan fed A.G.Doggart whose poor control seemed to have cost him the chance of a shot. But with the whole Blackburn defence drawn to the left in anticipation of a pass, Doggart suddenly unleashed a fierce ground shot which took everyone by surprise, not least the beaten Blackburn keeper.

Corinthians continued to dominate. A few minutes later, B.Howard Baker nearly scored with a wind-assisted goal kick while his opposite number Sewell was forced to make a smart save from Phillips who went on to squander another promising opening. On top of this, Corinthians were denied a strong claim for a penalty for handball. Shell-shocked Rovers strove to play the Corinthian way in the second half and had much more of the game. Howard Baker was repeatedly tested, McIntyre shot wide from close range and Mackay sent a powerful drive just wide of the upright. But Corinthians held on to claim a famous scalp. Even their 5-0 defeat at West Bromwich in the next round could not erase the memory of a wonderful amateur triumph.

Corinthians: B.Howard Baker; J.S.F.Morrison, A.G.Bower, I.B.Blaxland, C.T.Ashton, J.R.B.Moulsdale, K.E.Hegan, A.G.Doggart, F.N.S.Creek, A.H.Phillips, F.W.N.Nicholas.
Blackburn Rovers: Sewell; Rollo, Wylie, Roscamp, Healless, McKinnell, Crisp, McIntyre, Harper, Mackay, Byers.
Attendance: 20,000

'A crowd of nearly 20,000 people were absolutely pro-Corinthian from start to finish, though they were never aggressively demonstrative.'

The Times

10

Rochdale 1
Chilton Colliery Recreation Athletic 2

17 December 1925

The history of Rochdale FC is scarcely littered with great Cup exploits. They have never progressed beyond the fourth round and have fallen victim to, among others, Sutton Town, Altrincham (twice), Bangor City,

Grantham, Northwich Victoria and Telford United. Yet the most embarrassing day in their history was surely that when they succumbed to a miners' amateur side based in a village ten miles from Darlington.

They don't come any more romantic than Chilton Colliery Recreation Athletic. The team from the Northern Alliance had already surprised Carlisle (fellow non-Leaguers in those days) 2-0 in the first round but Rochdale were expected to prove a much tougher nut to crack. Rochdale were pushing hard for promotion from the Third Division (North) of the Football League (they eventually finished third, but were top scorers with 104 goals) and although the first match at Chilton had ended in a 1-1 draw, it was generally believed that the small pitch had hampered Rochdale and that the amateurs would be hard pushed to repeat the feat on the wide open spaces of Spotland.

If the Chilton players thought the FA Cup was all about glamour, then a drizzly Thursday afternoon in Rochdale must surely have shattered those illusions. With the possible exception of a head and shoulders of Graham Kelly, there are few less appealing sights in football.

A small gathering of hardy souls turned out to see Chilton make a lively start. Centre-forward Martin tried an ambitious overhead kick which Moody had to run out and save before, after only ten minutes' play, Rochdale were shaken by a goal. Chilton winger Scurr eluded Hopkins down the left, got to the by-line and pulled the ball back for Martin to score.

Rochdale were roused by the setback. A Whitehurst header was cleared by Richardson, then Guthrie dived to save from Hughes and, in the words of 'Soccerite' in the *Rochdale Observer*, 'fisted out splendidly a warm shot from H. Martin.' In the five minutes before half-time, Chilton suffered a cruel double blow. Centre-half Catterick, who had scored their goal in the first meeting, was penalised for a foul on Whitehurst just outside the box and Parkes rifled in the free-kick. Two minutes later, Catterick brought down Fergusson and was sent off.

Forced to play the entire second half with only ten men, Chilton's chances of survival looked slim, particularly when the referee awarded Rochdale a penalty. But the Chilton players protested and, after consulting one of his linesmen, the official changed his mind. Rochdale were making most of the running now and Guthrie saved well from Whitehurst. Then, with just eight minutes remaining, another Rochdale attack broke down. Dunn raced away on the right and slipped the ball inside to Thompson whose dipping, long-range shot sailed over the keeper's head, hit the inside of the far post and bounced into the net.

It was a goal completely out of the blue and one which left Rochdale precious little time to reply. Nevertheless, they nearly forced extra-time in the dying seconds, but Fergusson headed over from point-blank range.

Chilton Colliery's gallant run came to an end in the third round at South Shields and the club eventually folded in the 1940s. They never surpassed the glory that was Spotland. As for Rochdale, after hammering Crook Town 8-2 in 1927, they had to wait nearly twenty years, until 1945, for their next Cup tie victory. Over the years, Rochdale fans have learned to be patient.

Rochdale: Moody; Hopkins, Brown, Hillhouse, Parkes, Christie, Hughes, Bertram, Fergusson, Whitehurst, H.Martin.
Chilton Colliery Recreation Athletic: Guthrie; Owens, Hodgson, Richardson, Catterick, Taylor, Dunn, Thompson, A.Martin, Winter, Scurr.
Attendance: 1,500

'One of the football sensations of the season, the result was a staggering blow to the prestige of the Rochdale club and leaves one at a loss for an explanation.'

Rochdale Observer

11

Millwall 3
Huddersfield Town 1

8 January 1927

*W*ith three successive League Championships under their belt, Herbert Chapman's Huddersfield Town were the team everybody wanted to beat in the 1920s. Third Division (South) members Millwall had tried twice before but had been soundly defeated by the Yorkshire club in the Cup in both 1922 and 1923. So when the draw paired the clubs together for a third time, few gave the Lions much of a chance, particularly since high-flying Huddersfield had only lost two away games all season.

But Millwall had a plan to knock Huddersfield out of their aristocratic stride. They harried and hustled at every opportunity, giving the visiting defenders no time to settle. The result was a game which had all the skill and finesse of blow football.

'Millwall were off like hounds from the leash as soon as the whistle blew,' trilled the *Brockley News*, but it was something of a false start and, with better finishing from their star-studded forward line, Huddersfield could have put this third-round tie beyond reach in the first quarter of an hour. With Alex Jackson and Billy Smith menacing on the wings, Huddersfield tore the Millwall defence to shreds. Clem Stephenson fired just wide, Bryant made a desperate saving tackle to deny Smith and then George Brown fluffed his shot after good work from Jackson. Finally, on the half hour, Smith wriggled through again to lay on a gift for Brown and the England international duly side-footed home.

All Millwall had been able to muster at that stage was a harshly disallowed effort from Archie Gomm, yet within eight minutes of Brown's goal, they were level. Chance's cross was over-hit but the

Lions' other winger, Alf Black, retrieved it and slipped the ball inside to Wilf 'Peanut' Phillips who drove instantly into the corner of the net.

From that moment, the League Champions were completely over-run. The pocket megaphones carried by the Huddersfield supporters fell silent as their team's defenders proceeded to commit schoolboy blunders. On every attack, Millwall suddenly looked likely to score. They did not have long to wait. Early in the second half, Wadsworth failed to head clear a high ball and Gomm seized on the error to nod past the stranded Turner. With Wilson and Steel shadows of their normal selves, it was only a matter of time before Millwall added a third. It arrived midway through the half when two Huddersfield men miskicked a cross, leaving Black with a simple task from a few yards. Huddersfield finished a sorry rabble, Millwall's dominance being such that, after that first 15 minutes, Lansdale in the home goal had only one save to make, turning a shot from Cook onto a post.

Huddersfield recovered to finish runners-up in the League to Newcastle, while Millwall enhanced their reputation as giant-killers by reaching the sixth round where they lost to Southampton after a replay. Ten years later, they went one better, becoming the first Third Division team to reach the semi-finals, numbering among their scalps those of Chelsea, Derby and Manchester City. But none of these shocks was greater than their demolition of mighty Huddersfield.

Millwall: Lansdale; Fort, Hill, Amos, Bryant, Graham, Chance, Gomm, Parker, Phillips, Black.
Huddersfield Town: Turner; Goodall, Wadsworth, Steel, Wilson, Watson, Jackson, Cook, Brown, Stephenson, Smith.
Attendance: 36,000

'There was nothing picturesque about Millwall's methods. From the persistent manner in which they deliberately put the ball into the air, they might be said to have been unskilled. But the style was most effective.'

The Times

12

Brentford 2
West Ham United 0

2 February 1927

'The home ground was no doubt of the greatest value to Brentford, but it was a ground on which any team could have shown their best football. In spite of the weather the playing surface was extraordinarily good, and any team whose boot drill had been seriously attended to could find a firm and confident foothold.'

The Times

*A*h, *those were the days when a footballer's best friend was his tin of dubbin, not his agent, and when football boots were built for 90 minutes of mortal combat rather than the second act of Swan Lake. But from the way The Times correspondent waxed lyrical about Griffin Park, one wonders whether he mistakenly visited nearby Kew Gardens instead. One thing is certain – that Brentford's boot drill was accomplished enough to shock a West Ham side which only four years earlier had been at Wembley for the famous White Horse Cup Final.*

Even in 1927, West Ham were still good enough to finish sixth in the First Division. In the third round, they had overcome Spurs 3-2 in a thriller at Upton Park, as a result of which they were supremely confident of overcoming a Brentford team that was nothing more than mid-table fodder in Division Three (South). Indeed this was only the second season in which Brentford had been able to forego the chore of going through the qualifying rounds for the competition proper. They had, however, displayed a knack of goalscoring, putting seven past Isthmian Leaguers Clapton in the first round and four past Oldham in the third. Two of their previous rounds had gone to replays, and so it proved again here after Brentford had earned a creditable 1-1 draw at West Ham.

The second meeting took place at Brentford four days later. Dismayed by their lack of thrust in the first game, West Ham switched their England centre-forward Vic Watson to inside-left to form a potentially lethal left-wing combination with the lively Ruffell. Yet having made that tactical decision, they unaccountably proceeded to starve Ruffell of the ball so that the Hammers struggled once more to make any headway against a resolute Brentford rearguard in which centre-half Rae was outstanding.

With Douglas dangerous on the left, it was Brentford who made most of the early running. Allen met a Lane cross with a firm header, only to be denied by a brilliant full-length save from Hulton although Allen appealed in vain that the ball had crossed the line. West Ham replied with a good shot from Yews, capably dealt with by Ferguson, before Brentford made the vital breakthrough. Bellamy floated over a free-kick and as Watkins charged in, the ball fell to Lane who fired into the right-hand corner of the net despite a valiant effort from Hulton.

Lane, who had scored Brentford's goal in the first match, looked a constant threat but West Ham should have equalised when Campbell ballooned the ball high and wide from six yards following a neat pull-back by Yews. At the other end, Watkins also fired over from close range and with half-time approaching, Douglas kicked more ground than ball when only ten yards out.

Realizing the error of their ways, West Ham moved Watson back to centre-forward at half-time and, after surviving a scare right at the start of the second period, enjoyed their best spell of the match for the next quarter of an hour. Brentford seemed content to sit on their lead and nearly paid for it when Donnelly almost diverted a Watson shot into his own net. The Bees rode their luck, however, and made the game safe with ten minutes remaining. With West Ham committed to attack, Hendren played a quick free-kick through to Watkins who pulled the ball back for Allen to volley into the corner of the net.

Thus West Ham were left to concentrate on the League and, more importantly, the joys of boot drill.

Brentford: Ferguson; Donnelly, Butler, Beacham, Rae, Bellamy, Hendren, J. Lane, Watkins, Allen, Douglas.
West Ham United: Hulton; Hebden, Horler, Carter, Barrett, Collins, Yews, Earle, Campbell, Watson, Ruffell.
Attendance: 25,000

13

Guildford City 4
Queens Park Rangers 2

24 November 1928

B *eaten only once in the League and top of Division Three (South),*
Queens Park Rangers were hot favourites to overcome Southern
League Guildford City in their first-round encounter. Rangers had
toned themselves up for the battle ahead with a visit to the brine
baths at Southend while Guildford, whose previous victims had
included such stout opposition as the Aldershot Traction Company,
prepared for a record crowd at their St Joseph's Road ground.

Come the big day and City, winning the toss, elected to kick with the wind in the first half. They served early notice of their intentions when J. R. 'Tiger' Smith had a fifth-minute effort disallowed for offside. Indeed 'Goalkeeper' in the *Surrey Times* noted that City were frequently caught offside as 'Rangers adopted the one-back defence.' But City would not be denied. Cruickshank made progress down the wing and crossed to J. R. Smith who turned and shot for goal. 'Keeper Woodward held the ball for a fraction of a second but it dropped out of his hands and rolled almost apologetically into the net. 'Hats were thrown high in the excitement of the moment.' A minute later, Cruickshank nearly made it two.

Rangers' hopes of making greater headway in the second half with the wind at their backs were dashed in the opening minutes when

J. R. Smith took a pass from his namesake, Stan, and lobbed into the box where Hetherington glanced a neat header past Woodward. For the next 20 minutes, Rangers enjoyed their best spell of the match and reduced the arrears on 62 minutes when Goddard netted a rebound after Burns's shot had hit the post. Then a poor goal-kick from Drummond saw the ball strike a Rangers' forward and cannon back towards the goal. With Drummond hopelessly out of position, Ritchie reacted quickly to scramble the ball off the line. Boosted by this let-off, City won a 76th-minute free-kick. Viner's kick landed at the feet of Tinkler, whose shot was only parried for Hetherington to head home. Seven minutes later, the issue was put beyond doubt when J. R. Smith supplied Stan Smith who drove into the net with his weaker right foot. To their credit, Rangers came back and Drummond produced the best save of the match, tipping over a shot from Cockburn. From the resulting corner, Burns headed in but it was all too little, too late.

The final whistle produced scenes of excitement not seen in Guildford since the days of the Romans. Clearly overcome with emotion and possibly a nip of scotch, 'Goalkeeper' waxed lyrical in the *Surrey Times*. 'Never has such enthusiasm been seen on the ground as marked the sounding of the final whistle. The crowd rushed on to the pitch. Jack lifted his Jill on to his shoulder so that she could gaze in admiration and give her congratulatory greeting.' It had been quite a day.

Guildford City: Drummond; King, Ritchie, Stentiford, Viner, Cropper, Cruickshank, Hetherington, J.R. Smith, Tinkler, S. Smith.
Queens Park Rangers: Woodward; Sweetman, Young, McNabb, Cockburn, Neil, Coward, Burns, Goddard, Rounce, S. Smith.
Referee: Mr A.A. Small (Hampshire)
Attendance: 7,593

'**We are but Southern Leaguers weak! But we made Queens Park Rangers squeak! We put them out of the English Cup, And sold the London Press a pup!!**'

Guildford City's Hymn of Praise from the Surrey Times

14

12 January 1929

*A*s partings go, it was less obtrusive than Bobby Charlton's. Only 50 people bothered to turn up at Mansfield Railway Station to see the local football team off before their third-round tie at Wolverhampton. Indeed, the match was not even considered to be the town's most important sporting event that Saturday. That honour went to the annual show of the Mansfield and District Fanciers' Association whose array of rabbits and Rhode Island Reds occupied many more column inches than the fortunes of Mansfield Town.

Against this background of apathy, Mansfield set out to become the first Midland League team to reach the fourth round of the FA Cup. The last to reach the third round were Worksop Town in 1923 who, after a memorable goalless draw at White Hart Lane against Spurs, contrived to lose the replay (also at White Hart Lane) 9-0. Mansfield were not without hope. Wolves were only a moderate Second Division outfit while Town lay fourth in the Midland League, behind Lincoln City Reserves, Notts County Reserves and Gainsborough Trinity, but with games in hand. Furthermore, they had been drawn away in every round so far and had successfully accounted for Ardsley Athletic (after a replay), Shirebrook and Barrow.

If Wolves were expecting Mansfield to sit back, they were in for a surprise. The visitors made a lively opening, captain Chris Staniforth leading by example with a shot which Lewis turned for a corner. From the kick, Morris darted in but fired wide. Wolves looked jittery at the back but gradually they began to settle and forced Arthur Staples, the Nottinghamshire cricketer, into three important saves. Then, after 26 minutes, Mansfield launched a devastating counter-attack. Cooke broke clear down the left and the only team-mate able

34

to keep pace with him was former Queen's Park, Third Lanark, Leicester and Forest right-winger McLachlan, said to be the fastest player in the Midland League. Cook looked up, saw that McLachlan had moved into the middle and sent over a perfect low cross, leaving the Scot with the easiest of tasks to score.

Wolves tried to retaliate but their attacks lacked any form of cohesion. Weaver did have a chance just before the break but his control let him down. The *Nottingham Evening News* reporter was clearly not enjoying the game. Perhaps his Bovril was cold or maybe he wished he had been sent to cover the Fanciers' Show. Whatever the case, his comments were scarcely complimentary. 'Kick and rush was the order of the day,' he wrote, 'and at this, Mansfield excelled.' As the match drifted to a conclusion, he added: 'The game was decidedly ragged, skill being entirely absent.' He was no Brian Moore.

Wolves' late rally, like their previous efforts, came to nought and so the conquering heroes returned to Mansfield. By now, the town had woken up to their team's achievement and a crowd of 4,000 had gathered at the station (although it is possible that most were waiting for a late train). 'THE WHOLE TOWN REJOICING' rang out the headlines. There was even greater excitement when Mansfield were drawn at Highbury in the fourth round but a 2-0 defeat spelt the end of their dreams. And the following year, they lost in the first round at home to a Cheshire County League outfit called Manchester Central. It was back to the Rhode Island Reds.

Wolverhampton Wanderers: Lewis; Williams, Shaw, Brown, Hollingworth, Kay, W. Richards, Green, Weaver, Marshall, Baxter.
Mansfield Town: Staples; Anthoney, Jackson, Kay, Chambers, McKenna, McLachlan, Staniforth, Morris, Kerry, Cooke.
Referee: Mr S. Tilston (Cheshire)
Attendance: 21,837

'Frequently Wolverhampton's efforts aroused ironical laughter. Their forwards were distinctly crude in most that they attempted.'
Nottingham Evening News

15

26 January 1929

'The Biscuits and the Blades. Twenty-two good men and true, trained to the minute, eager for the blast of the whistle which enables them to get off the mark, under the critical gaze of thousands of spectators, at least one of whom walked all the way from the cutlery town and arrived weary, with one arm broken in an accident on the way and lost nothing thereby either in cash or morale.'

Reading Football Chronicle

The Darlington experience of 1920 should have taught Sheffield Wednesday never to underestimate the opposition. But by the end of that decade, they were a much stronger side. In the last week of January they held a five-point lead at the top of the First Division table and were well on their way to their first League championship for 25 years. Such was their prowess that they went on to retain the title in 1930. Yet all great teams have the occasional hiccup and Wednesday's was a fourth-round tie at Reading, a club struggling to avoid relegation from the Second Division.

Reading themselves had reached the semi-finals two years earlier and had already accounted for Spurs, also then a Second Division side, in the third round. Nevertheless, it was a major surprise when Wednesday fell at Elm Park.

In fairness, Wednesday were handicapped by an ankle injury to centre-forward Allen in the first half which left him hobbling for the rest of the match. With their prolific leading scorer present in mind only, the Wednesday forwards were a pale imitation of their usual selves. The first half was a tepid affair, producing just three goal attempts – two from Wednesday's Jimmy Seed, one of which was well saved, and the third from Reading centre-forward Johnstone shortly before the changeover.

If Reading thought they had been denied a penalty in the first half when Blenkinsop hauled down the marauding Johnstone, the injustice was balanced out after the break when home right-back Inglis went unpunished for a clear handling offence at a corner.

It seemed that Wednesday's class would finally begin to tell in the last half-hour. Duckworth in the home goal was forced into a series of daring saves although he was well beaten by an effort from Hooper which struck the bar.

Then, on 75 minutes, against the run of play, Reading stole the winner. Hunter fed Oswald out on the left but, to the surprise of the Wednesday defenders, the winger cut inside and released a square pass to the unmarked Johnstone who steadied himself before beating Brown from close range. Wednesday rallied valiantly and Marsden went close but the final whistle heralded a famous victory. Reading were unable to reproduce their heroics in the next round, going down 3-1 at home to Aston Villa, but they had reminded Wednesday that it could be tough at the top.

It must have been a long walk home for that poor supporter.

Reading: Duckworth; Inglis, Smith, Chandler, Messer, Meads, Goodwin, McDonald, Johnstone, Hunter, Oswald.
Sheffield Wednesday: Brown; Walker, Blenkinsop, Strange, Leach, Marsden, Hooper, Seed, Allen, Gregg, Rimmer.
Referee: Mr A. G. Price (London)
Attendance: 29,248

16

Newark Town 2
Rotherham United 1

29 November 1930

*T*he quiet Nottinghamshire market town of Newark has never exactly been a hotbed of football. To most of the residents, 'soccer' is a word you get ten points for at Scrabble (20 if you land on a double word square). Yet even Newark Town had their moment of Cup glory when the Muskham Road ground was packed to the rafters to see 'The Blues' knock out Rotherham United in a first-round tie 64 years ago.

True, Rotherham were no great shakes, struggling at the wrong end of Third Division (North) with a defence which had so many leaks they needed a plumber rather than a manager. At the end of the season, only Merthyr Town had conceded more goals in the entire Football League. Then again, Newark were only a modest Midland League team but a pitch more suited to growing rice than playing football bridged any gulf in class there might have been between the two sides.

Rotherham made the mistake of trying to play a short-passing game in the quagmire conditions whereas Newark preferred to rely on the hefty boot. Early on, Rotherham had a remarkable escape. Hoddinott's effort eluded visiting keeper Harris and trickled along the goal-line. Speed seemed certain to score but the cloying mud prevented him from reaching the ball even though he was never more than a yard from it as it continued its tantalising journey. In the 23rd minute, Speed made amends, gathering an overhead kick by Roseboom and holding off Jackson to score. Fourteen minutes later, he struck again. The hard-working Hoddinott's angled drive was dropped by Harris and Speed followed up to put Newark two ahead. Rotherham replied within a minute, Murden heading in a Sellars cross.

At half-time, Rotherham changed their kit and the comfort of a clean pair of shorts appeared to inspire them to greater heights with Sellars sending over a stream of dangerous crosses. However, it was Newark who came closest to scoring when Morton's effort was ruled not to have crossed the line before Harris scooped it away. Rotherham's fightback was handicapped by an injury to Gray, sustained in the 65th minute. Badly concussed, he was reduced to the role of a passenger and twice had to leave the field for treatment. Displaying a distinct lack of compassion, the *Newark Advertiser* wrote: 'Though he returned against the advice of his trainer, his pluck was his only asset. He moved to outside-right where he staggered about like a drunken man, and was again taken off the field before the end.'

Gray's valour proved in vain. Rotherham were unable to force an equaliser and the final whistle revealed that Newark had a wounded hero of their own. Lowe had played throughout with a blistered heel, an injury which, declared the same *Newark Advertiser* proudly, 'would have prevented a less plucky man from turning out.' They were big on pluck in Newark. The team themselves were skinned alive 6-0 at Crystal Palace in the next round.

Newark Town: Best; Pearson, York, Stanniland, Bennett, Lowe, McLean, Roseboom, Speed, Hoddinott, Morton.
Rotherham United: Harris; Jackson, Freeman, Skull, Bratley, Whitworth, Sellars, Gray, Hick, Murden, F.C. Wheeler.
Referee: Mr Manderfield (Grantham)
Attendance: 2,700

17

Exeter City 3
Derby County 2

10 January 1931

*D*erby's young, aggressive team were fancied by many to win the
Cup in 1931. Built around the talents of England international
*Sammy Crooks and prolific goalscorer Jack Bowers (his 37 for the
season set a club record), they were lying third in Division One with
five away wins to their credit. The Derby line-up included George
Mee, brother of Bertie, who, although also on County's books, never
made the first team. All in all, a third-round visit to an Exeter side
which was not exactly setting Division Three (South) alight did not
seem too daunting a prospect. But City were unbeaten at home since
September and when a flock of seagulls flew over St James's Park
shortly before kick-off (a seagull was the club mascot), Exeter knew
it was to be their day.*

After 'selections by the Exeter City Military Band enlivened the
period of waiting', the teams took the field and Exeter swarmed
straight on to the attack. Purcell was only inches wide and then left-
winger Doncaster lobbed over the keeper, only to see his effort strike
the crossbar. A goal had to come and it duly arrived in the 12th
minute. Doncaster beat Cooper and crossed. Purcell's shot hit a
defender but, with the Derby defence again all at sea, Varco pounced
to give City a deserved lead.

As befitted their status, Derby stormed back and laid siege to the
home goal. Crooks was denied by full-back Baugh, Davies saved a
header from Stephenson and Bowers twice went close with headers.
Somehow Exeter managed to survive until half-time. Even the
Military Band were living on their nerves.

Yet after such stout defensive work, Exeter conceded an equaliser within a minute of the restart. Ramage swept the ball upfield to Crooks who steadied himself before delivering a pinpoint cross for Bowers to head in. Everything seemed to go wrong for Exeter now. Right-half 'Nobby' Clarke was taken off suffering from concussion and then right-back Baugh was the victim of a dubious tackle by Mulloch. With Baugh also off the field, Exeter were down to nine men, but happily Baugh was able to return a few minutes later.

Amazingly, after 65 minutes Exeter regained the lead. Varco's shot was sailing harmlesly wide until Armfield diverted it back into the net. This gave the ten men fresh heart and Doncaster rattled an upright. Then on 75 minutes, Purcell's free-kick brought a weak clearance from Derby keeper Kirby and as the ball dropped, Houghton chested it over the line. Kirby promptly made amends by tipping a Purcell shot over the bar as Exeter continued to defy the odds but when Bowers headed home another Crooks cross on 83 minutes, the stage was set for a grandstand finish. Derby threw everything at Exeter in those closing minutes and came within a whisker of salvaging a replay, Barber being forced to clear off the line with the referee about to blow for full-time.

Few neutrals could deny that gallant Exeter deserved their victory on the day. In the wake of their famous triumph, City went on to account for Bury and First Division Leeds before going down to Sunderland in a sixth-round replay. To this day, Exeter have never bettered that Cup run.

Exeter City: Davies; Baugh, Miller, Clarke, Dennington, Barber, Armfield, Purcell, Varco, Houghton, Doncaster.
Derby County: Kirby; Cooper, Collin, Nicholas, Jessop, Mulloch, Crooks, Stephenson, Bowers, Ramage, Mee.
Referee: Mr Small
Attendance: 16,500

'I thought all along the team could do it. I said this morning they would do it and naturally I am delighted that they have done it.'
Exeter manager Billy McDevitt, celebrating his team's victory

41

18

Folkestone 1
Norwich City 0

26 November 1932

'The Folkestone players are to be congratulated upon the splendid way they played and they deserve our thanks for the wholesome recreation they provided.'

> *The Mayor of Folkestone, Alderman J. W. Stainer,*
> *himself a Folkestone player in the 1880s*

Folkestone player/manager Harry Warren wore an air of confidence. It was, he said, derived from a recent victory over the might of Tunbridge Wells Rangers. Harry was obviously easily pleased. Few others in this corner of Kent shared his optimism. Anyway they were more concerned with the continuing rumours about the possible building of a Channel Tunnel.

Norwich presented formidable first-round opposition for the Southern League club. Among the high fliers in Division Three (South) of the Football League, City's success was based around their resolute defence. Unbeaten away from home since losing at Cardiff on 3 September, they had conceded just eight goals in seven away League games – and four of those had been at Ninian Park.

But one of Folkestone's number had old scores to settle. Their long-serving goalkeeper Goodman had been in the Folkestone side which suffered qualifying round defeats at the hands of Norwich in 1923 and 1924. In the process, he had conceded five goals. He was determined to make amends here.

In front of the massed ranks at Cheriton Road, the Wasps, as Folkestone were known, chose to kick with the wind in the first half and soon put Norwich under pressure. Keeper Robinson brought off a great save to deny Edwards and then Sparke, who had been ill all week and, according to the Folkestone Herald, was 'not feeling too grand', shot just wide. Goodman was called into action to deal with a high dropping effort from Murphy before Folkestone were presented with a golden opportunity in the 17th minute when Smith was penalised for a foul on the combative 'Pat' Havelock. Full-back Rossiter stepped up to take the spot kick but crashed it against the bar from whence it rebounded to safety.

The lead was not long delayed. Eight minutes later, former Tunbridge Wells Ranger Percy Richards took a pass from 'Pat' Havelock and climaxed a 50-yard run with a low shot into the corner of the net.

Norwich hit back but their best forward, Burditt, squandered a chance after Ramsey had squared the ball to him and then Goodman brought off a fine save from Scott. City's hopes of getting back into the game at the start of the second half never materialised as they were pinned on the ropes by the buccaneering Folkestone forwards. For 20 minutes, Norwich could hardly get out of their own half. 'Pat' Havelock, who 'unsettled the City backs with quite legitimate forcefulness', was proving a veritable handful alongside his brother Harry. Robinson tipped over a good effort from Harry and then 'Pat' twice went close with headers. On another occasion, Richards flashed the ball across the face of the goal but nobody was able to provide the finishing touch.

As Folkestone began to tire in the latter stages, Norwich surged forward in a bid to salvage their reputation. But Goodman would not be beaten. He went down well to smother a shot from Burditt at the foot of the post and then watched a strike from B. Robinson hit the side netting. In a rare breakaway, Black fired wide of a gaping goal but it proved of little consequence and soon the Mayor was practising his victory speech. He had another to make two weeks later when Folkestone put out visiting Newport County 2-1. In the end, it took the might of First Division Huddersfield to halt the little Kent club's progress that winter.

19

Walsall 2
Arsenal 0

14 January 1933

When the third-round draw paired Herbert Chapman's all-conquering Arsenal with little Walsall, the result seemed a foregone conclusion. For while the Gunners sat proudly on top of the First Division, Walsall were languishing in tenth place in Division Three (North), ten points off the leaders Chester. The Press called Arsenal the '£30,000 aristocrats', comparing them to Walsall whose team cost £69. Indeed, Arsenal had spent more on their boots than Walsall had on their team. What's more, the Midlanders had gone a month without a win and had only once progressed beyond the third round of the FA Cup.

Chapman clearly thought Walsall posed little threat. He 'rested' three internationals – Hapgood, John and Lambert – although the official line was that they were either injured or stricken by a 'flu epidemic', and dropped winger Hulme. The reshaped line-up included three youngsters – Black, Walsh and Warnes – making their debuts, while Sidey had made only one senior appearance. But the feeling was that even if Chapman himself had turned out, Arsenal would not be troubled to win.

Perhaps Chapman should have heeded the warning signs. After all,

Arsenal had seen their six-point lead at the top of the table eroded to two following successive defeats at Sheffield Wednesday and Sunderland. On the morning of the match, *The Times* said of Arsenal: 'They should beat Walsall easily,' before adding cautiously, 'but when there are so many strange faces, one never can tell.' One of the strange faces, Charlie Walsh, was so nervous before the game that he put on his boots before his socks!

The Walsall pitch was narrow and muddy. Arsenal adapted to neither. *The Times* reported that 'Walsall's football was better, much more virile, and so roused to the occasion that from the start they had Arsenal in difficulties.' Chapman's newcomers looked sadly out of their depth. Tommy Black, a young Scot replacing Hapgood at left-back, was unable to cope with speedy Walsall winger Coward; Warnes, preferred to Hulme, was largely anonymous; Sidey was outclassed; and Walsh got no change out of the Saddlers' tough-tackling centre-half Leslie. Even the visitors' star forwards, David Jack and Alex James, made little headway against the resolute Walsall rearguard. In truth, only Cliff Bastin emerged from the nightmare with his reputation intact.

Walsall, who themselves were without their most accomplished half-back, Langford, tore into Arsenal from the off. Ball and Coward posed a constant threat and Arsenal keeper Moss was forced into useful saves from Alsop and Lee. Arsenal's best effort of the first half was a fine shot from Bastin shortly before the interval.

With the slope in their favour in the second half, it seemed that Arsenal would finally take control. Warnes was presented with a good chance but delayed and was dispossessed by Salt, Jack was robbed in front of an open goal when Walsh managed to get in his way and Walsh himself missed a decent opportunity. But only Bastin seriously tested Cunningham, 'a vigilant but by no means overworked goalkeeper.'

Having survived these attacks, Walsall broke out and on the hour, the unthinkable happened when Gilbert Alsop headed in Lee's cross. Then five minutes later, the hapless Black hauled down Alsop and

Billy Sheppard converted the resultant penalty.

The second goal completely knocked the stuffing out of Arsenal. They offered little resistance in the remaining 25 minutes and were fortunate not to lose by a bigger margin. At the final whistle, the Walsall players were carried off shoulder high by their jubilant fans. When the scoreline filtered through, it created such shock waves that some newspapers checked with their reporters to make sure it was not the wrong way round!

Chapman wasted no time in punishing the miscreants. So incensed was he by Black's reckless tackle on Alsop that he refused to allow the youngster to return to Highbury. Within a week, Chapman had sold him to Plymouth. Walsh was transferred to Brentford at the end of the month and Warnes departed to Norwich in the summer.

Although Arsenal recovered to lift the first of three consecutive League Championships, for years the mere mention of 'Walsall' was enough to send a shiver down the spines of the most hardened Gunners' fans.

Walsall: Cunningham; Bennett, Bird, Reed, Leslie, Salt, Coward, Ball, Alsop, Sheppard, Lee.
Arsenal: Moss; Male, Black, Hill, Roberts, Sidey, Warnes, Jack, Walsh, James, Bastin.
Referee: Mr A. Taylor (Lancashire)
Attendance: 11,150

'We had a corner and their full-back, Black, was marking me. He didn't get up. The ball was just a big plum pudding that day and I headed it off my forehead straight into the corner of the net. I'd been watching Dixie Dean play for England.'

Walsall match-winner Gilbert Alsop

Carlisle United 1
Cheltenham Town 2

9 December 1933

'We go to Carlisle full of hope. We realise we are up against a stiff proposition in meeting a League side like Carlisle on their own ground, but at the same time we invariably produce our best form on opponents' soil.'

Cheltenham Town captain George Blackburn, previewing the tie

*P*laying in the Birmingham Combination, Cheltenham Town were enjoying only their second campaign as a semi-professional club. Having trounced Athenian Leaguers Barnet 5-1 in the first round of the Cup, they faced a tougher prospect at Carlisle who, although only mid-way in the Third Division (North), had been beaten just once at home all season.

Fortified by the gift of a lucky horseshoe from Gloucester weight-lifter Joe Price, the Cheltenham team headed north for a match which was to end in uproar amidst scenes of crowd unrest.

There was no indication of any discontent in the first half as Carlisle dominated proceedings. Cheltenham keeper Davis pulled off a great save from Slinger, Kennedy drilled wide from close range and Stevenson had a shot deflected for a corner before United finally broke the deadlock in the 44th minute. Slinger received the ball some 20 yards out and, although surrounded by defenders, somehow found sufficient space to lash the ball past Davis.

Yet within four minutes of the restart, Carlisle were stunned by a Cheltenham equaliser. Yarwood created the opening for Smith to score with a low angled shot. Carlisle remained on top but Williams marshalled the non-Leaguers' defence superbly, saving the day with a timely clearance after Blake had struck the bar with a powerful shot. Then Davis was forced to keep a watchful eye on a swerving strike from winger McBain.

Carlisle's world went flat in the 80th minute when the ball did the same. With the new ball, they immediately had fervent claims for a penalty for handball turned down. In the ensuing protests, referee Warburton sent off their centre-half Kennedy. Worse was to follow. A minute from time, Cheltenham broke away. Yarwood fed Hill who tried to tap the ball wide of the oncoming Wolf. As Wolf ran out, United skipper Bob Bradley, making a desperate attempt to clear, intercepted but merely succeeded in steering the ball into his own net. There was still time for one last act of drama. In an almighty scramble, the ball and Cheltenham keeper Davis finished up in the back of the net but, to the disgust of the home supporters, Mr Warburton awarded a free-kick to Cheltenham on the goal-line.

At the final whistle, several hundred Carlisle fans vented their anger by swarming onto the pitch and making a bee-line for the referee who had to have a police escort to the safety of the dressing-room. As dejected Carlisle counted the gate receipts of £371 19s 9d, exultant cries of 'Bravo, Cheltenham' could be heard in the streets of Gloucestershire that evening. Cheltenham Town made national headlines. The *Observer* summed it all up. 'How few knew that there was a club so useful at Cheltenham!' The euphoria must have gone to their heads. They haven't beaten a League club since.

Carlisle United: Wolf; Bradley, Legge, Blake, Kennedy, Clark, McBain, Gray, Slinger, Stevenson, Turner.
Cheltenham Town: Davis; Jones, Williams, Lang, Blackburn, Goodger, Payne, R.Smith, Yarwood, Evans, Hill.
Referee: Mr R.K. Warburton (Bolton)
Attendance: 7,437

21

Margate 3
Crystal Palace 1

14 December 1935

'The Margate players have been taking walks by the sea this week and tonight the team will be the guests of Dreamland Cinema at the first performance.'

Isle of Thanet Gazette on the Friday before the game

*W*hen talk of the FA Cup turns to Margate, the chances are it will alight on the 1971 meeting with Bournemouth which Margate lost by the worrying margin of 11-0, Ted MacDougall scoring nine of the goals. However, Kent fans with bus passes may recall instead the glorious Cup run of 1935-36 when first Queens Park Rangers and then Crystal Palace were despatched from the competition at Hartsdown.

Apart from the stroll along the beach (not something out of the Howard Wilkinson manual) and the trip to the cinema (they saw 'Public Hero Number One', a tense thriller starring Chester Morris and Lionel Barrymore – if they'd waited another week, they could have seen 'The Bride of Frankenstein'), Margate's preparations did not all run according to plan. There was widespread dismay at the increase in admission prices – up to 3s 6d for the East Stand and 3s for the West Stand – although entry to the remainder of the ground remained at a more modest 1s. And they lost the services of centre-forward Clarke, 'struck down by an epidemic of boils'. One would have thought that such an embarrassing complaint would at least have ensured that he would not have been too closely marked during the match.

In those days, Margate acted as a nursery club to Arsenal and among the good luck messages pouring into the town prior to the second-round tie with Palace was one from Highbury. Not that Margate expected to have to rely on luck. They had won all of their home games in the Southern League that season, scoring 24 goals and conceding just two. Palace were a moderate ninth in Division Three (South) although they possessed a lively forward line and were to finish second highest scorers in the division with 96 goals, six fewer than champions Coventry. Their line-up also contained a former Margate player, full-back Booth.

Unaccustomed as they were to conceding goals at home, Margate received a nasty shock in only the eighth minute. Palace, kicking down the slope, launched a swift attack through Dawes. 'Keeper Preedy dived to save but in the ensuing melee, Blackman pounced to score. Birtley missed a glorious chance to increase Palace's advantage and then Preedy did well to deny Dawes before Margate delighted the record crowd with a 35th-minute equaliser. A free-kick for handball some 35 yards out appeared to pose little threat but right-half Evans had other ideas. Before Palace could organise themselves, he took the kick and shot through a crowd of players into the net past the surprised Dunn.

With the slope in their favour, Margate dominated the second half, beating Palace at their own game by using short inter-passing movements rather than resorting to the long ball so often favoured by non-Leaguers. Eight minutes after the break, the tricky Farr put Davie through but just as he was about to shoot, he was fouled by keeper Dunn. Despite heated protests from the Palace players, the referee awarded a penalty which Evans duly converted. Two minutes later, the wing-half completed a remarkable hat-trick. Dunn raced out to clear but stumbled as he did so. The ball fell to Evans who slotted into the vacant net from 25 yards. Dawes tried to inspire a Palace recovery but Margate were in no mood to let their lead slip.

And so the Kent club reached the third round where they lost 3-1 at Blackpool. Alas, their victory over Palace received little recognition. For it so happened that on the same day, Ted Drake was busy scoring all seven goals for Arsenal at Aston Villa.

22

Accrington Stanley 3
Blackburn Rovers 1

20 January 1937

*T*he glamour of the FA Cup singularly managed to bypass Accrington. From 1896 until their sad demise in 1962, they were more accustomed to facing the might of Oswaldtwistle Rovers and Horden Colliery Welfare than Everton or Arsenal. So a plum third-round draw with illustrious neighbours Blackburn offered a rare opportunity to bring a little excitement to Peel Park.

Rovers were by no means at their peak. The previous season had seen them relegated from the top flight for the first time in their history and they now occupied nothing more than a mid-table berth in Division Two. Even so, that was many rungs above Accrington. When they had finished ninth in Third Division (North) in 1936, it was only the fourth time Accrington had ever been placed in the top ten. It seemed a false dawn as the 1936-37 season left them anchored to the foot of the table by the middle of September. Then the re-signing of centre-forward Bob Mortimer from Portsmouth brought about an improvement. He scored 33 goals in 37 League games to help Stanley to a respectable final position of 13th.

Mortimer carried his exploits over into the Cup, scoring in the first-round victory over Wellington Town and then helping Stanley to overcome visiting Tunbridge Wells Rangers in the second. The 1-0 winning margin over the little Kent Leaguers scarcely suggested that Blackburn had much to fear, but Mortimer had other ideas.

The clubs had last met in the competition in 1909 when Blackburn romped home 7-1 but this time Stanley made the short journey to Ewood Park on the back of three straight wins, an almost unparalleled feat. For their part, Rovers had lost five of their previous six games. Over 31,000 saw Mortimer strike twice to earn Stanley a 2-2 draw and a replay four days later.

Somehow over 11,000 squeezed into Peel Park for the replay. The Scratching Shed, as the old Burnley Road stand was affectionately known, was bursting at the seams. With a plum tie at Maine Road awaiting the winners, Stanley remained unchanged but Blackburn were forced to make a number of changes.

Given the advantage of the slope, Rovers roared onto the offensive and stunned the home side with a fourth-minute goal, Calladine meeting a right-wing cross from Sale to score via a post. As Blackburn continued to dictate the play, Alf Robertson in the Accrington goal was relieved to beat out a drive from Sale and then see a Calladine drive fly over the bar. Stanley gradually began to get into the match and should have equalised when Billy Tyson could only head wide after Mortimer's shot had struck the inside of a post. Encouraged by this, Stanley launched a succession of high crosses into the Blackburn box but Frank Christie held firm at the heart of the visitors' rearguard. Behind him, keeper Pratt was less confident and it was his blunder, shortly before half-time, which allowed Accrington to equalise. Under no pressure whatsoever, he fumbled a low centre, leaving Mortimer with a simple task.

Remarkably, Stanley maintained the pressure in the second period with Walter Reynolds giving Walter Crook a torrid time. The nearest they came to snatching a winner was a header from Mortimer which flashed over the top.

Extra-time was a different matter. The cloying pitch turned the match into a trial of strength and Stanley's superior fitness proved decisive. On 104 minutes, a mistake by Christie enabled Mortimer to fire Accrington ahead. As the crowd sensed a real shock, Walter Rivers put the issue beyond doubt with five minutes remaining. Although Stanley lost 2-0 at Maine Road, they had made their mark on that season's competition. Blackburn had certainly been impressed, so much so that they soon snapped up Mortimer and Tyson.

The result was that the following season, Accrington finished bottom of the table and had to apply for re-election. Another fine mess, Stanley.

Accrington Stanley: Robertson; Gregg, Reeday, Nisbet, Craven, Andrews, Reynolds, Rivers, Mortimer, Tyson, Mee.
Blackburn Rovers: Pratt; Lanceley, Crook, Whiteside, Christie, Pryde, Bruton, Lee, Sale, Calladine, Baxendale.
Referee: Mr G. Hewitt (St Helens)
Attendance: 11,636

23

Chelmsford City 4
Southampton 1

7 January 1939

*F*ew teams in the history of the FA Cup appeared less capable of springing a giant-killing act than Chelmsford City's 1939 vintage. With only five wins all season, they were slumped in 20th spot in the Southern League, below such powerhouses as Plymouth Argyle Reserves, Arsenal III, Newport County Reserves and Tunbridge Wells Rangers. Yet from the rubble of this disastrous season, they somehow contrived to humiliate Second Division Southampton. And the only surprise to those who braved the elements at New Writtle Street on that January afternoon was that Southampton escaped so lightly.

En route to the third round, Chelmsford had disposed of Barking,

Fords Sports, Crittall Athletic, Romford, Dulwich Hamlet, Kidderminster Harriers and Darlington. Now, in readiness for the visit of Southampton, they headed for the brine baths at Southend, hoping no doubt that the salt would not have the same effect as on Queens Park Rangers at Guildford ten years earlier. Anticipating a large crowd, Chelmsford placed additional seats around the cinder track to raise the capacity to 18,000. They could have saved themselves the trouble. For the appalling weather meant that only the brave ventured out.

The pitch, if that's not too strong a word for it, consisted of a thick layer of sludge over frost-bitten soil. The *Essex Chronicle* reported that, prior to kick-off, Chelmsford captain Alan Sliman was presented with a large doll, attired in the club colours of claret and white, which he nursed for a few seconds before distributing it to other members of the team. Presumably the doll was not of the inflatable variety.

Like many League teams before and since, Southampton's undoing was their inability or reluctance to adapt their tactics to the state of the pitch. They stuck rigidly to a close-passing game which inevitably became bogged down in the mud. By contrast, Chelmsford relied solely on the big boot, followed by a mass cavalry charge. This so unnerved the visiting defenders that in the event, only Warhurst in the Southampton goal prevented a rout.

To be fair, Southampton had been hit by injuries. Henderson, a late replacement at full-back, struggled throughout against the elusive Coulter while young Carnaby, another deputy, was unable to contain Palethorpe who had already notched ten goals in Chelmsford's Cup campaign. Of the Southampton team, only Brophy played up to form. Saints' inside-left Briggs had an early chance but shot wide with just Davison to beat and from then on, it was all Chelmsford.

The first goal came on 12 minutes. A Bell-Palethorpe-Coulter move produced a goalmouth melee which ended with Southampton centre-half Carnaby putting the ball into his own net. Warhurst then made a point-blank save from Landells as Chelmsford piled on the pressure. 'Jones was playing magnificently,' wrote the *Essex Chronicle*, 'and once, when he was illegally brought down, there threatened to be a "scene".' From Hamlet, perchance?

Chelmsford soon doubled their lead. Wright's shot was parried by Warhurst, and Palethorpe followed up to score despite a gallant attempt by the keeper to retrieve the situation. After 35 minutes, Southampton briefly got back into the game when Holt netted from a 20-yard free-kick but four minutes later, the two-goal margin was restored. Coulter relieved Southampton pressure with a break down the left and crossed for Palethorpe to beat Warhurst comfortably. In the minutes before half-time, Chelmsford nearly added two more, Coulter being guilty of a glaring miss and then Wright producing an air shot in front of goal.

It was the same story in the second period. As his defence went AWOL, poor Warhurst was left hopelessly exposed. Lady Godiva had more cover. After making great saves to thwart Bell and Wright, Warhurst pulled out another brilliant stop to deny Wright. But this time, the ball ran to the unmarked Coulter who made it 4-1. At that point, Chelmsford seemed to declare, satisfied with their afternoon's work, and no further embarrassment was inflicted upon the visitors.

Such excitement greeted the result that one supporter unwisely entered into print with a poem entitled 'The City's Alphabet'. For the benefit of literary buffs, the entries included:

'I is for Itching '
For Saturdays to come
J is for Jones
Oh Boy! What a plum' and
M is for Moments
We're held in suspense
N is for Nonsense,
Our boys are not dense.'

He was clearly struggling by then. So were his beloved City two weeks later in the fourth round when they crashed out 6-0 at Birmingham. It is not known whether our author re-wrote his ditty.

24

Colchester United 1
Huddersfield Town 0

10 January 1948

*T*he story of Bob Curry was that of which FA Cup legends are made. Seriously wounded at Dunkirk, he feared that his playing days were over but recovered to score the goal which gave Southern League Colchester an epic victory over First Division Huddersfield in 1948.

Colchester United had only been formed in 1937. Lying eighth in the Southern League, they had already seen off Banbury Spencer and Wrexham when the third-round draw brought Huddersfield to Layer Road. Whilst not the force they were in the 1920s, the Yorkshiremen still paraded a formidable line-up, headed by their recent expensive signing, Peter Doherty, the Northern Ireland international inside-forward, who had gained a Cup winners' medal with Derby in 1946. Furthermore, goalkeeper Hesford and left-half Boot were survivors from Huddersfield's last Wembley appearance when they lost narrowly to Preston in 1938.

Huddersfield were 1-8 favourites to defeat Colchester but they had reckoned without United's shrewd boss, Ted Fenton. He put his players on a diet of oysters, perhaps reasoning that even if they couldn't beat Huddersfield they could mate with them. He also had Huddersfield watched in a League game at Portsmouth and

Members of the Joyce Grenfell Appreciation Society cheer Colchester to a famous victory.

afterwards staged a private trial match at Layer Road to exploit the weaknesses he had seen. As a result, Fenton was supremely confident. 'Let 'em all come, that's our motto,' he said, 'and at Layer Road, we are not one little bit overawed by the reputations of our famnous opponents.' One other good omen was that both of Colchester's previous victims had played in red and now, owing to a colour clash, Colchester borrowed West Ham's reserve strip of blue shirts with white cuffs and collars while Huddersfield took the field in a change strip of red.

From the kick-off, it was soon apparent that Huddersfield were distinctly unhappy on the cramped Layer Road pitch. There was no room for Doherty to demonstrate his skills and if he did manage to find a yard of space, he was quickly shackled by the tough-tackling Colchester defenders, notably right-half Harry Bearryman. And with Albert 'Digger' Kettle subduing Huddersfield's dangerous left-winger Metcalfe, the visiting forwards rarely found any rhythm.

Instead it was Colchester who made the running with Dennis Hillman and Len Cater a constant threat on the wings. In the centre, Arthur Turner, a member of Charlton's Cup Final team of 1946 but playing here with a poisoned foot, came close to scoring on four separate occasions and was also unlucky to have a 'goal' disallowed. Cater was narrowly off target with a fierce drive while Huddersfield's best chance fell to, and was squandered by, Whittingham. Apart from that, United keeper Harry Wright, who was nursing a swollen finger, was scarcely troubled.

The winning goal came on 69 minutes. A mazy run by Kettle was brought to a halt when he was felled three yards outside the penalty area. Allen's free-kick, delivered low and hard, was too hot for Hesford to hold and he could only push it out as far as Curry who took his time before firing into the net just inside the post.

So impressed were Huddersfield with Colchester's performance that after the game they made tentative enquiries about Bearryman and Kettle. In the fourth round, United beat Second Division Bradford Park Avenue (who played in red) 3-2 before going down 5-0 at Blackpool (who didn't) in round five. But the Cup run had achieved its aim and two years later, United were elected to the Football League. Their new-found status did not mean that their days of giant-killing were over. For then there was Leeds…

Colchester United: Wright; Kettle, Allen, Bearryman, Fenton, Brown, Hillman, Curry, Turner, Cutting, Cater.
Huddersfield Town: Hesford; Hayes, Barker, L. Smith, Hepplewhite, Boot, C.Smith, Glazzard, Whittingham, Doherty, Metcalfe.
Referee: Mr G. Reader
Attendance: 16,000

'When the ball came to me, it was spinning wildly so rather than risk a first-time shot, I steadied myself before shooting.'

Colchester goal hero Bob Curry

25

Yeovil Town 2
Sunderland 1

29 January 1949

*I*t was the result which shook the nation. Soccer writers believed they had been conditioned to Cup shocks by the exploits of the likes of Walsall and Colchester but nobody was prepared for this. What possible hope could Yeovil Town, sixth from the foot of the Southern League, have against mighty Sunderland, eighth in Division One, and whose numbers included the 'clown prince of football', Len Shackleton, at £20,050 the country's most expensive player? But the pundits had overlooked two factors: Yeovil's Cup pedigree and their infamous slope at The Huish.

Yeovil & Petters United, as they then were, had been upsetting League clubs since 1924 when they knocked out Bournemouth. Crystal Palace, Exeter, Brighton and Bury had subsequently found themselves reluctant additions to the list. But the only First Division team to visit Somerset, Liverpool in 1935, had returned to Merseyside with a comfortable 6-2 victory under their belts. So why should this year be any different?

For a start, Yeovil possessed a wily leader in Alec Stock, one of the game's great characters and communicators. Before the third-round tie with Bury, the national Press, in their eagerness for stories, had lapped up Stock's description of the 10ft slope at The Huish. The *Daily Graphic* printed it as 14ft and every subsequent paper added a couple more feet. As Stock himself said: 'By the time match-day came around, everyone must have had the idea we played on the north face of the Eiger!'

Bury were duly vanquished 3-1 and the legend of the slope persisted. For the Sunderland game three weeks later, the build-up again centred on the slope with the Yeovil players doing their best to get away from it all by taking the week off work and sampling the brine baths at Weston-super-Mare. On the morning of the match, *The Times* sounded a cautionary note. 'Nor need we doubt that Sunderland, for all their tradition and the class of players such as Shackleton, Robinson and Watson, know full well what to expect on the sloping ground of humble little Yeovil Town. Yeovil, with everything to gain and nothing to lose, are in an enviable position.'

Queues started forming outside the ground at 8am. There was a sell-out crowd but Yeovil's biggest problem was accommodating the 100 or so journalists who descended on the town to cover the match. With nowhere to house them, the club had to borrow an array of desks from a nearby junior school. The sight of 15-stone journalists, fortified by expense account lunches, squeezing into seats designed for seven-year-olds was something to behold…

All vantage points were taken. Spectators unable to acquire a ticket perched on neighbouring rooftops or crammed ten to a window. As the teams ran out, eyes focused on Len Shackleton, team-mate Jackie Robinson who, ten years earlier had earned Sheffield Wednesday a Cup replay against Yeovil, Alec Stock and then an unfamiliar figure, Yeovil's rookie goalkeeper Victor Dyke, a 23-year-old solicitor's clerk called up for only his second game in the first team as a last-minute replacement for the injured Stanley Hall. How would he react to such an occasion?

There was little chance to find out the answer in the first half since the majority of the play took place at the other end. Yeovil attacked from the start with right-winger Bobby Hamilton running opposing left-back Barney Ramsden ragged. The chances began to come. Mapson in the Sunderland goal saved twice in quick succession from Eric Bryant and Hamilton and was then caught out by Hamilton's long high cross but, fortunately for the visitors, neither Bryant nor Ray Wright could reach it. The siege continued. Bryant had a 'goal' disallowed – he had flicked it in with his fist – Stock and Bob Keeton shot just wide and Willie Watson cleared off the Sunderland line with Mapson beaten.

It seemed that Yeovil's pressure would go unrewarded until they were awarded a free-kick in the 26th minute. Hickman's kick was flicked on by Wright for Stock to shoot first-time beyond Mapson. It was a timely moment for the player-manager to score his first of the season.

Just before the interval, Yeovil nearly got a second. Wright had the goal at his mercy but was brought down just outside the box by centre-half Hall. There was no professional foul in those days so Yeovil received nothing more than a free-kick which came to nothing.

On 62 minutes, Sunderland equalised. Dyke, who had otherwise dealt capably with everything, made his one mistake of the match. He jumped to save from Ramsden but as he did so, he fell over Sunderland centre-forward Ronnie Turnbull and dropped the ball at the feet of Robinson who promptly tucked the chance away, scarcely able to believe his good fortune. Undeterred, Yeovil hit back and Ralph Davis ran 50 yards to feed Bryant who, to the despair of the crowd, shot high over the bar from close range. Towards the end of the 90 minutes, Sunderland came more into the game. But the home half-back line of Keeton, Blizzard and Collins held firm, restricting them to one dangerous assault which saw right-winger Len Duns go agonisingly close.

In the years immediately after the War, extra-time was played in the first match in order to conserve energy and avoid lost working days and so the fans got an additional 30 minutes for their money. By now, the ground was engulfed in dense fog and Sunderland, led by the menacing Turnbull, at last began to exercise control. But just when it looked as though Yeovil had shot their bolt, Len Shackleton, of all people, made the mistake which was to catapult the Somerset team into the history books. The tie was in its 104th minute when Shackleton, the crowd pleaser, did exactly that. Juggling the ball on the half-way line, he proceeded to play a sloppy pass back towards his own goal. It was intercepted and pushed through by Wright for Bryant to run on and score.

The Huish erupted. It did so again ten minutes later when the referee blew for a Sunderland free-kick and the crowd ran on to the pitch, thinking it was all over. There was a delay of several minutes while the pitch was cleared for the remaining six minutes' play. Yeovil managed to hold out and when the final whistle did go, the *Western Gazette* described 'jubilant scenes reminiscent of VE Day.'

Sunderland manager Bill Murray was gracious in defeat. 'There has been too much talk about the pitch,' he said. 'There is nothing in it. Our boys may have found it a little strange at the start, but the truth of the matter is that they were beaten by a better team.' As Yeovil's fame spread, reports came in of a terrific cheer at the Pavilion Theatre, Bournemouth, that evening when a member of the cast sporting a huge green and white rosette announced on stage: 'Roses are red, violets are blue, Sunderland one, Yeovil two.' There was less to celebrate a fortnight later when the part-timers went to Old Trafford to see if they could repeat their heroics. They couldn't, and crashed 8-0 before a crowd of 80,000. But Yeovil would live to fight another day.

Yeovil Town: Dyke; Hickman, Davies, Keeton, Blizzard, Collins, Hamilton, Stock, Bryant, Wright, Hargreaves.
Sunderland: Mapson; Stelling, Ramsden, Watson, Hall, Wright, Duns, Robinson, Turnbull, Shackleton, Reynolds.
Referee: Mr A.W. Smith (Aldershot)
Attendance: 17,100

'Len Shackleton gave the ball away because he was dead scared of our right-half Bob Keeton. Bob pushed the ball through to Nick Collins and he moved it on to Ray Wright. A little push forward to me and I ran past their centre-half, got just inside the box and put the ball into the bottom left corner of the Sunderland net. I think what really won the match for us was the way Alec Stock wound us up beforehand. He was such a marvellous talker – he could have told us black was white and we'd have believed him.'

Yeovil match-winner Eric Bryant

26

Gateshead 1
Liverpool 0

10 January 1953

*I*t was only three years earlier that Liverpool had stepped out at
Wembley prior to their Cup Final defeat by Arsenal but such
occasions mean little on a wintry January afternoon in Gateshead.
The fog on the Tyne was particularly bad that third-round day.
Indeed across the river at St James's Park, Newcastle's tie with
Swansea was abandoned after only eight minutes.

Both sides were going through an indifferent patch. Gateshead had
picked up just three points from their previous four games (three of
them at home), their most recent setback being a 2-1 defeat by
Southport. By no stretch of the imagination was a home defeat by
Southport the ideal preparation for a big Cup tie. Liverpool manager
Don Welsh also had problems. His team were in the wrong half of the
First Division and he made five changes from the side beaten by
Stoke the previous week, including giving a debut to left-half
Saunders. Nevertheless, their line-up still contained three
internationals, among them that tricky Scottish winger Billy Liddell.

Few of the 15,000-plus crowd at Redheugh Park could see much of
the action and the general consensus of opinion was that there wasn't
a lot to see. Following a first-minute scare, in which visiting keeper
Crossley failed to hold a centre from Smith, Liverpool began to settle
down without ever making much impression on the Third Division
(North) side's defence. This was built around brothers Jack and
Tommy Callender, two figures hewn from granite. Williams and Jack
Smith had chances for Liverpool, while Liddell drifted in and out of
the fog like Jack the Ripper without causing anything like as much
havoc. Tired of the constraints imposed by Cairns, Liddell later
switched wings but enjoyed no better fortune on the left.

By then, Gateshead had taken control, forcing a series of corners. They thought they had made the breakthough in the 73rd minute when Brown found the net direct from a free-kick but the effort was mysteriously disallowed. It was as much as the players could do to find the referee, let alone argue with him. Finally, six minutes from time, one of their corners paid dividends. Campbell swung over the flag-kick and Ian Winters emerged from the fog to head firmly past Crossley.

L. O. Hetherington summed up the performance in the following day's *Sunday Sun*. 'The success of the Redheugh team was not of the fluke type. The whole Liverpool attack, after their early touches of craft and method as befitted their status, were completely subdued by the grand home half-back line and it was one-way traffic to the Liverpool goal.'

Encouraged by this unexpected triumph, Gateshead went on to win at Hull and Plymouth, thus reaching the sixth round for the only time in their history. There, they were edged out 1-0 at home by eventual losing finalists Bolton.

Gateshead: Gray; Cairns, March, J. Callender, T. Callender, Brown, Ingham, Smith, Wilbert, Winters, Campbell.
Liverpool: Crossley; Lambert, Moran, Heydon, Jones, Saunders, Payne, Baron, Smith, Williams, Liddell.
Referee: Mr F.B. Coultas (Hull)
Attendance: 15,193

27

10 January 1953

Gateshead's giant-killing feat was somewhat overshadowed by the efforts of Isthmian Leaguers Walthamstow Avenue on that same afternoon in 1953. For in defeating Stockport County, Avenue became the first amateur side to reach the fourth round of the Cup since the Corinthians in 1929.

Avenue, who had roasted Northampton 6-1 in 1936, were renowned Cup fighters. They had already defeated Wimbledon (also members of the Isthmian League in those days) and Watford on the way to reaching the third round in 1953 so the visit of Stockport to East London held few terrors for them. After all, County were nothing more than an average Third Division (North) side. But there was an old score to settle. For Stockport had knocked Avenue out of the Cup back in 1938. The amateurs' captain that day was Jim Lewis and now his son, Jim junior, was about to lead the attack on the revenge mission.

Yet the hero of the hour turned out to be inside-right Dick Lucas, a frail-looking fellow who played with a special plaster support to brace his spine. Earlier in the season, he had displaced his spinal disc and had been urged to quit playing altogether. But, like Colchester's Bob Curry before him, he was determined to soldier on.

Quoting from the handbook of soccer cliches, this was definitely a game of two halves. The first was dominated by the Amateur Cup holders who, with a modicum of good fortune, could have been four ahead by the break. As it was, they had to settle for two. Twice they struck the woodwork before finally taking the lead. The first goal came when Trevor Bailey beat two men out on the right and crossed for Ken Camis to hit the bar. But this time, there was no escape for

Dick Lucas (hoops) beats the forlorn figure of Stockport keeper Boles to put Walthamstow Avenue 2-0 up.

County and the onrushing Lucas headed in the rebound to the delight of the crowd at Green Pond Road, a setting which sounds more like something from 'Wind in the Willows' than the FA Cup. The second stemmed from a long pass by left-half Saunders which found Hall in a promising position. The ball was moved on to Lucas who, from just inside the box, shot to the left of Boles and into the back of the net.

Stung into action, Stockport proceeded to pound the home goal in the second half. But Doug Young and Lou Brahan held firm at the back, the latter doing a particularly sound job in shackling County centre-forward Jack Connor, his division's leading scorer. Avenue meanwhile were restricted to breakaways. Lewis was very much a lone raider but his presence commanded the attention of no fewer than three County defenders, thereby allowing wingers Bailey and Camis plenty of room.

On 74 minutes, County reduced the arrears, Moran netting from six yards following a goalmouth scramble. This led to an agonising final quarter of an hour. Such was the tension that Avenue supporters were rumoured to be chewing each other's fingernails. They were down to the knuckles in the final minute when home keeper Stan Gerula saved the day with a brilliant stop to deny Cocker.

So Avenue gained their revenge but the real reward was to come with the fourth-round draw – a trip to Old Trafford. There was to be no repeat of the Yeovil massacre as a Lewis goal earned the amateurs an incredible 1-1 draw. In the replay at Highbury, Lewis bagged two more but United ran out 5-2 winners. The fairytale was over.

Walthamstow Avenue: Gerula; Young, Stratton, Harper, Brahan, Saunders, Bailey, Lucas, Lewis, Hall, Camis.
Stockport County: Boles; Bell, McCullock, Murray, Wilmott, Patterson, Cocker, Moran, Connor, Bodle, Oliver.
Attendance: 9,500

'Dick Lucas was the inspiration of the brilliant A's frontline and claimed the goals with complete assurance. It is, however, invidious to single out any member of this superlative A's side for individual mention. For this was no one-man effort, but a co-ordinated team, exuding a spirit and determination from every one of the blue-shirted stalwarts.'

'Heron' of the Walthamstow Guardian on the victory over Stockport

28

Great Yarmouth Town 1
Crystal Palace 0

21 November 1953

'Not even the chastened Palace followers, who long before the end had lost their pre-match enthusiasm, could have denied the Town's right to advance into the next round.'

Yarmouth Mercury

There was some unrest in the seaside town of Great Yarmouth when it was announced that Crystal Palace would be visiting Wellesley Road for a first-round Cup tie. The previous year, Wrexham had come to Norfolk, prompting complaints from many of the assembled throng that they had been unable to see the match properly. Anticipating another large crowd (it was to be a ground record), Yarmouth boldly resisted offers to stage the game at Norwich City's Carrow Road and instead embarked on an ingenious campaign to improve spectator conditions. Hundreds of fish boxes (a commodity in ready supply locally) were placed on the terraces for extra elevation while seats and forms were borrowed from Yarmouth racecourse, Gorleston FC, who were without a game that day, and even the Wellington Pier. Everyone would be able to get a clear view this time.

Top of the Eastern Counties League with eight wins from 13 games, Yarmouth faced a Palace team in the top half of Division Three (South). However the Londoners were by no means immune to giant-killing. In addition to Margate in 1935, they had also gone out of the Cup to Bath City, Yeovil Town and, only the previous year, little Athenian Leaguers Finchley. Yarmouth had never previously beaten a League club. This was to be their finest hour.

The only goal of the game came as early as the sixth minute. Town player/manager Jack Bradley began a move which led to Plunkett lofting the ball into the box. With the Palace defenders mesmerised, winger Rackham ran in at the far post to head his first goal for the club.

From then on, it was nearly all Palace. Driven on by Cecil Andrews, who rejoiced in the topical nickname of 'Archie', at times they threatened to overrun Yarmouth but spoiled their slick approach work by trying one pass too many. When they did get a sight of goal, their finishing was generally woeful although both Leslie Fell and Ernie Randall were foiled by the woodwork. Palace claimed they should have had an equaliser when Town keeper Canning scooped the ball off the line but referee Ling, who controlled the 1951 Cup final, waved play on. Palace were at their most dangerous in the period around half-time but Bullock remained solid at the heart of the home defence while Arnold was 'admirably restrained' at full-back.

Slowly Palace ran out of steam and it was Yarmouth who finished the stronger with Rackham and Cutting troubling Bailey on a number of occasions. Nevertheless, they were indebted to a late headed clearance by Arnold with Canning beaten.

At the final whistle, those who had stood on fish boxes to watch the minnows raced on to the pitch to engulf their heroes. Great Yarmouth would see nothing like it again until the Beverley Sisters appeared in summer season.

Great Yarmouth Town: Canning; Rowlands, Arnold, Kirk, Bullock, Newby, Rackham, Cutting, Plunkett, Bradley, Green.
Crystal Palace: Bailey; Choules, Edwards, Willard, Briggs, Andrews, Fell, Thomas, Randall, Foulds, Devonshire.
Referee: Mr W. Ling (Stapleford)
Attendance: 8,944

29

Port Vale 2
Blackpool 0

20 February 1954

This was the day the people of the Potteries had yearned for – the return to their bosom of their most famous son, Stanley Matthews, with the Blackpool side which, nine months earlier, had lifted the Cup in that most dramatic of all finals, against Bolton.

Although they occupied a lofty position in Division One, Blackpool knew that Port Vale, clear leaders of Third Division (North), would be no pushover. In the wake of their Wembley triumph, Blackpool's 1954 Cup campaign had been a stuttering affair. It had taken them six matches to reach the fifth round – four against Luton in the third, and a replay to overcome West Ham in the fourth. Vale's run had begun at

Darlington the previous November and had progressed via Southport, Queens Park Rangers and Cardiff. The tie in Wales had been a stormy affair with irate City fans hurling snowballs at the referee.

Above all, Vale were a formidable home side. They had conceded only one goal at Vale Park all season – and that was on 5 September, nearly six months previously.

During the week prior to the Blackpool match, it had rained non-stop and groundstaff had used sacks to dry out the pitch. But the day itself was sunny. Matthews' return plus the prospect of an upset caused a tremendous clamour for tickets. They were quickly sold out and only appeals from the police and the club directors finally dispersed the crowd. The thousands who could not get in listened to a loudspeaker commentary relayed to them especially for the occasion while hordes of children managed to watch the game from the perilous perch of a 40ft wall which overlooked the ground.

Port Vale goalkeeper King makes an unorthodox catch to deny Blackpool. When he opened his eyes, Vale were in the sixth round.

Blackpool fielded seven of their Cup-winning team but they were without Stan Mortensen. Another absentee was their mascot, a live duck, which was unable to make the journey because of fowl pest restrictions. Judging by the state of the pitch, the duck may have been a greater loss than Mortensen.

After a Vale fan in top hat and shorts had entertained the masses by dribbling a rubber ball before kick-off (people were easily pleased in those days), the teams came out to a tremendous roar. All eyes were on Matthews but he appeared hesitant and out of sorts. He was largely anonymous, poorly served by his inside-forwards Taylor and Brown, both of whom were harried throughout by the Vale wing-halves, Mullard and Sproson. As *The Times* put it: 'He was a stranger in a friendly land.' Only twice did Matthews threaten. One mazy run through the mud presented Taylor with a chance but the latter fired straight at King and later, receiving a rare good pass, he accelerated clear, only for Cheadle to get across brilliantly to save the day.

It was the pace of Bill Perry on the other wing which offered Blackpool most hope but even he missed the one clear chance which came his way when he shot wide just before half-time with only King to beat. For the rest, although they enjoyed long periods of possession, Blackpool rarely looked dangerous.

By contrast, the Vale forwards proved a real handful. Utilising the wide pitch, they played fast, constructive football, stretching the Blackpool defence to the limit. Blackpool's England international centre-half Harry Johnston was hard pushed to contain the powerful, wandering Hayward while Leake and Griffiths were infinitely more effective than their opposing inside-forwards, keeping tricky wingers Askey and Cunliffe constantly supplied. Quite simply, Vale were quicker to the ball and stronger in the tackle.

The goals came in a devastating ten-minute spell in the first half. After 15 minutes, Cunliffe's corner was superbly headed home by Albert Leake. Then Griffiths and Cunliffe combined to send Hayward marauding down the left. As the Blackpool defence froze in hope of an offside flag, it was Leake again who raced in to flick Hayward's diagonal pass beyond hesitant Scottish international goalkeeper George Farm.

Vale were worthy winners. They went on take the divisional title in a canter (losing just three games all season) and to reach the semi-finals of the Cup, only the second side from the Third Division to do so, following Millwall in 1937. There, Albert Leake scored again but West Bromwich Albion scraped through 2-1 before defeating Preston at Wembley. It took a good side to beat Port Vale that year.

Port Vale: King; Turner, Potts, Mullard, Cheadle, Sproson, Askey, Leake, Hayward, Griffiths, Cunliffe.
Blackpool: Farm; Shimwell, Frith, Fenton, Johnston, Kelly, Matthews, Taylor, Stephenson, Brown, Perry.
Referee: Mr H. Jackson (Leeds)
Attendance: 40,500

'The wonder of it all grew out of a blue sky and even the harsh, scarred countryside of the Potteries, where vast kilns point upwards like chubby fingers, took on a kindly, gentle look.'

The Times

30

Bishop Auckland 3
Ipswich Town 0

12 January 1955

J*ust about the most famous of all amateur teams, Bishop Auckland's finest giant-killing performance in the FA Cup was their dismissal of Second Division Ipswich from the 1954-55 competition.*

When the draw took the Bishops to Suffolk, few gave them much of a chance despite Ipswich's poor League form. Yet only an 84th-minute own goal by the Northern Leaguers' centre-half Corbett Cresswell enabled Ipswich to scramble a replay. The second match was scheduled to take place four days later but, seeing three inches of snow on the Kingsway pitch, Ipswich manager Scott Duncan not surprisingly wanted the game postponed. 'Nonsense,' replied the Bishops, 'we have played in far worse conditions.' Indeed, to the hardy folk of the north-east, such weather is considered positively spring-like.

The match went ahead and Duncan made a number of changes from the first game, dropping inside-left Ted Phillips (later to become a Portman Road folk hero) and, even more suprisingly, leading scorer Tom Garneys. The Bishops were at full strength although there had been a doubt as to whether McKenna would be able to obtain leave from the RAF, an appropriate job for a winger!

It was neither a game for the purist nor the faint-hearted. The wind howled across the narrow little ground while the players struggled to keep their feet on the treacherous surface. A ground pass was more likely to form a snowball than an attack.

Playing with the advantage of wind and slope, the Bishops must have expected to make early inroads yet it was Ipswich who looked the more composed side in the first half, only to be repeatedly denied by Cresswell, Marshall and the offside flag. Sharratt in the home goal was also called upon to make some important saves although his handling was decidedly erratic, partly due to his puzzling refusal to wear gloves for the occasion. When Sharratt was beaten, after 22 minutes, Garneys' replacement Grant delayed the shot for so long that Cresswell was able to make a saving tackle.

Curiously it was when the elements were no longer in their favour that the Bishops began to take command. On the hour, flying winger McKenna suffered a leg injury. The trainer wanted him to come off but McKenna demanded to be allowed to stay on and, in the true romance of the Cup, responded with the opening goal five minutes later. Long-serving right-half Bob Hardisty, who the *Auckland Chronicle*'s fashion correspondent noted was wearing nylon pants for the game, took a free-kick some 35 yards out. Oliver's firm header was only palmed out by Welsh international keeper Jack Parry and McKenna limped in to nod into an empty net. Ipswich folded dramatically and Bishop Auckland took full advantage. After 70 minutes, Lewin made it 2-0, taking a pass from Oliver and shooting wide of Parry from the edge of the box. There was no holding the Bishops now and the inevitable third came five minutes from time, Major netting with a sweet strike from 18 yards. By the final whistle, Ipswich were a shambles and it came as little surprise to their fans when they were relegated at the end of the season. Little could they have dreamed that seven years later, their team would be crowned League Champions.

Bishop Auckland: Sharratt; Marshall, Stewart, Hardisty, Cresswell, Nimmins, McKenna, Lewin, Oliver, Major, Edwards.
Ipswich Town: Parry; Malcolm, Feeney, Myles, Rees, Parker, Reed, Crowe, Grant, Callaghan, McLuckie.
Referee: Mr G. McCabe (Sheffield)
Attendance: 9,000

'I was surprised Ipswich made so many changes from the team they fielded on Saturday. As a result, their forward line was definitely weaker. Their wingers were not supplied with the ball to the same extent as in the first match.'

Stewart, the Bishop Auckland captain

31

York City 3
Tottenham Hotspur 0

19 February 1955

B ishop Auckland's reward for defeating Ipswich was a home tie with York City, riding high in Third Division (North). York had already won 2-0 at Blackpool in the third round and, with the aid of *two goals from the splendidly-named Arthur Bottom, duly knocked out the gallant amateurs 3-1. This set up a fifth-round tie with Tottenham Hotspur.*

Half of the Spurs team were internationals, among them England full-back Alf Ramsey, but the team of many talents had been sliding perilously close to the First Division relegation zone, the decline only arrested by the recent purchase of Irish international Danny Blanchflower from Aston Villa for £30,000. York, on the other hand, had no worries about form. They had suffered just two defeats in their previous 23 games and were a formidable proposition at Bootham Crescent. To add to Spurs' discomfort, the pitch was a mixture of ice, snow and slush and had only been passed playable after the York groundstaff had spent the morning shovelling away the layer of snow.

It would be easy to blame the pitch for Tottenham's misery but York were no kick-and-rush side. Unlike some minnows, with whom the ball spends about as much time on the ground as it does in basketball, York liked to play to feet. They beat Spurs fair and square, with superior football. The architect of this famous triumph was speedy left-winger Billy Fenton who gave poor Ramsey a torrid afternoon. When Ramsey said in 1966 that he wanted to do away with wingers, perhaps it was Billy Fenton he still had in mind...

Yet there was little hint of a shock early on. In the 11th minute, Ramsey set up a smooth attack down the right. The move was carried on by Walters and Duquemin for George Robb to shoot home from five yards.

York hit back with a vengeance. On 29 minutes, Fenton drew Ramsey right across the pitch with him on a long diagonal run before cleverly backheeling to Hughes wide out on the right. Hughes quickly cut inside and crossed for Wilkinson to head into the top corner of the net. Unbelievably, a minute later York were in front. Bottom popped up in midfield and laid on a chance for Wilkinson. His fierce shot was parried by Reynolds and Fenton followed up to score.

Apart from one fine header from Len Duquemin, it was all York after that. They launched attack after attack, never for a moment contemplating sitting back on their lead. Only Reynolds kept the score down. Out-thought and outpaced, Spurs were forced to pass square. Blanchflower worked hard and displayed some neat touches but his forwards were unable to make any headway against the likes of Brown and Howe. *The Times* wrote: 'Long before the finish all that we saw were the cherry-red shirts of York. Tottenham, in white, had disappeared, merged in the wintry scene, and melted away like the early flurry of snowflakes that fled as the sun came out to smile on a great and unquestioned triumph.'

The icing on the cake came in the 81st minute when Wilkinson fired the third goal from Fenton's centre. The final whistle brought a 'grey wave of muffled figures breaking over the field to chair their champions off.' Like Port Vale the year before, York went on to make the semi-finals. No Third Division side has come nearer to reaching Wembley, for they took Newcastle to a replay which they eventually lost 2-0. Spurs' manager Arthur Rowe, creator of the celebrated 'push and run' team, was badly shaken by the York defeat. Shortly afterwards, he was taken ill and resigned his post. The new boss, Jimmy Anderson, promptly dropped Ramsey and by the start of the 1955-56 season, Ramsey had taken over as manager at Ipswich.

York City: Forgan; Phillips, Howe, Brown, Stewart, Spence, Hughes, Bottom, Wilkinson, Storey, Fenton.
Tottenham Hotspur: Reynolds; Ramsey, Hopkins, Blanchflower, Clarke, Marchi, Walters, Baily, Duquemin, Brooks, Robb.
Referee: Mr G. Gibson (Manchester)
Attendance: 21,000

'**Ramsey was unable to cope with Fenton who, with Hughes on the opposite flank, was a constant threat. Ramsey, indeed, was sometimes not in the same county as Fenton showed him his heels.**'

The Times

32

Derby County 1
Boston United 6

10 December 1955

*F*ew Cup giant-killers had as much incentive to win as Midland Leaguers Boston United when they made the trip to the Baseball Ground for a second-round tie in 1955. For there were no fewer than six former Derby players in the Boston side – Reg Harrison, who actually played for the Rams in the 1946 final, brothers Geoff and Don Hazledine, Ray Wilkins, Dave Miller and keeper Ray Middleton, Boston's player/manager. All had been discarded by the Third Division (North) hotshots and put out to graze in rural Lincolnshire, so each had a point to prove. As an added inducement, Boston's landowner president, Frank Pitcher, promised each of the players a pheasant from his shoot if they won. It certainly made a change from the usual offer of a day trip to Skegness.

But the likelihood of Mr Pitcher's game birds ending up on a footballer's dinner table, smothered in tomato ketchup and dwarfed by a mountain of mushy peas, seemed highly remote. After all, Derby, third in the table, were unbeaten at home all season and were averaging over three goals per game at the Baseball Ground. The previous week, they had thrashed Darlington 6-2 to become the highest scorers in the entire Football League. For their part, Boston had only ever once progressed beyond the second round of the Cup – and that was back in 1926.

However, Boston did their homework. They watched Derby three times and knew that County wing-halves Mays and Ryan loved to attack at every opportunity. So, Boston set out to exploit the space behind the pair. They also knew that Derby relied heavily on the service provided by schemer Jesse Pye, a £5,000 signing from Luton. Accordingly, Don Hazledine was detailed to close Pye down at every opportunity.

The plan worked like a dream and, with Snade also blotting out Derby's dangerous winger Cresswell, Boston soon had both sets of supporters in a state of total disbelief. They opened the scoring in the 26th minute. When Harrison's shot rebounded to him off a Derby defender, he slipped the ball to Wilkins who fired past Webster in the home goal. Seven minutes later, Webster fumbled a shot from Geoff Hazledine who quickly latched on to the loose ball to make it 2-0.

It seemed that Derby had been given a lifeline when Don Hazledine was harshly penalised for hands and Pye slotted home the 36th-minute penalty, but three minutes before half-time, Birkbeck further exposed County's defensive frailties with a splendid header from Howlett's cross.

Although they were now down to ten men (McDonnell having gone off injured in the 44th minute), surely Derby would sort things out in the second half. And for a while they attacked with purpose. But they were still hopelessly vulnerable to Boston's rapid breaks and, after Wilkins had struck the bar with a fierce drive, the same player raced through the middle, drew a defender and slipped the ball to Geoff Hazledine who scored comfortably. That was after 61 minutes and three minutes later, the move was repeated, Geoff Hazledine taking Wilkins' pass to net from an acute angle. Finally, on 76 minutes, a Harrison cross eluded the miserable Webster for Wilkins to claim his second and Boston's sixth. The Derby fans were left to reflect on what is still their heaviest home defeat in the Cup this century and on how unwise the club had been to dispense with the services of the Boston Six so readily.

After this sensational result, a Boston bookmaker reported taking 17 bets on United to win the Cup at 2,500 to 1. The locals weren't getting too carried away though – the stakes ranged from 1s to 10s. Even so, you could buy a lot of Spam for 10s in those days. Like most bookies, he was soon in the money. The third-round draw took Boston to Tottenham where they lost 4-0.

Derby and Boston met again in the Cup in 1974 and, by a curious twist of fate, this time it was Derby who won 6-1 away from home.

Derby County: Webster; Barrowcliffe, Upton, Mays, McDonnell, Ryan, Cresswell, Parry, Todd, Pye, Powell.
Boston United: Middleton; Robinson, Snade, D. Hazledine, Miller, Lowder, Harrison, G. Hazledine, Wilkins, Birkbeck, Howlett.
Referee: Mr E. Jennings (Stowbridge)
Attendance: 23,757

'No, I shall not go to Derby because I can't stand the strain of seeing the United humiliated.'

Ardent Boston supporter before the 1955 tie

33

Notts County 1
Rhyl 3

5 January 1957

*I*magine Arsenal basing their game plan on the word of Ronnie Corbett? Or Jackie Charlton taking advice from the Nolans? Maybe it's not as far-fetched as it sounds, for Rhyl's secret 'scout' before their third-round Cup tie with Notts County in 1957 was none other than popular comedian/band leader Vic Oliver.

It so happened that Vic Oliver was appearing at the time in panto at the Theatre Royal, Nottingham, with 'dame' Harry Shiels, a fervent Rhyl supporter. A matinee performance prevented Shiels from seeing the Cup match but he wrote to Rhyl saying that Vic Oliver had watched County twice that season and that his advice to Rhyl was to swing the ball about and tackle quickly. It may not have been quite as detailed as one of Don Revie's dossiers but it certainly did the trick.

Cheshire County Leaguers Rhyl had enjoyed a degree of Cup success in the past. They had reached the third round once before, in 1927, putting out Stoke and Wrexham before losing to Darlington. Notts

County were having a rough time of it in the Second Division but had not been beaten by a non-League team in the Cup since Southern League Bristol Rovers knocked them out in 1913.

Around 1,500 Rhyl supporters travelled to Nottingham in two specially decorated trains. Also on board were the Rhyl Silver Prize Band (pity the poor passenger sat next to the trombonist) who proceeded to play the Welsh National Anthem as the Rhyl players ran out at Meadow Lane. To add to the festivities, visiting fans planted a succession of leeks in the centre circle before kick-off. They really knew how to enjoy themselves in those days.

Both teams sprang selection surprises. Notts gave a debut to 18-year-old left-winger Peter Bircumshaw, a free scorer in the reserves, while playing his first game for Rhyl was left-back Ken Reynolds. But the greatest shock of all was the omission of Rhyl's long-serving centre-forward Don Spendlove who had scored 536 goals for the club.

Even so, Rhyl paraded plenty of experience, with a number of ex-League players in their line-up, whereas County were a fairly raw bunch, particularly up front. The difference was to prove decisive.

As early as the fifth minute, the dangerous Henry Williams headed against the underside of the bar for Rhyl but it was not until the 20th minute that the visitors took the lead. A long pass from Donaldson landed at the feet of Henry Williams but before he could shoot, County right-half McGrath barged him off the ball. A free-kick was awarded on the edge of the box and County formed a defensive wall. For some reason, keeper Linton elected to position himself behind the wall, leaving Henry Williams to lob the ball into the unguarded corner of the net.

With an advantage to protect, Rhyl became a shade rattled and conceded a string of free-kicks. On 37 minutes, Notts equalised. 'Keeper Hanson fumbled Wylie's header from Wills' driven cross and young Bircumshaw poked the loose ball into the net. For a while, Notts held the upper hand but the turning point in the match was a controversial incident on the hour. As Henry Williams ran on to

Roberts' through ball, Notts defender Russell was adjudged to have pushed him. Despite home protests, the referee pointed to the penalty spot. Billy Hughes calmly placed the ball in the left-hand corner of the net but was then ordered to retake it because a Notts player had encroached! Hughes was unshaken by this novel interpretation of the laws and put his second effort in precisely the same spot.

Notts were now distinctly second best. They had a rare chance when Reynolds cleared off the line from Wills but six minutes from the end, the unmarked Graham Meakin put the issue beyond doubt by heading home Henry Williams' cross at the far post.

Two days later, Notts sacked their manager, George Poyser. Rhyl didn't fare much better, crashing 3-0 at Bristol City in the fourth round. If only Vic Oliver had taken his show to Bristol…

Notts County: Linton; Southwell, Cruickshank, McGrath, Russell, Loxley, Lane, Wylie, Wills, Carver, Bircumshaw.
Rhyl: Hanson; Spruse, Reynolds, Roberts, Rogers, Donaldson, Hughes, Russell, J.Williams, H. Williams, Meakin.
Referee: Mr H. Webb (Leeds)
Attendance: 16,231

'Well done, Rhyl. You gave our Second Division team a real football lesson with a wonderful display of fast open football. On this day's display Rhyl were one of the best teams seen on our ground this season. We would also like to add a word of praise for the very fine playing of the Rhyl Silver Prize Band – music that really set the hearts on fire.'

A letter to the Rhyl Journal
from 'a bunch of Notts County supporters on the 2s side'

34

Bournemouth & Boscombe Athletic 3
Tottenham Hotspur 1

16 February 1957

*T*wo years after York, Spurs found themselves the victims of
another giant-killing sensation, this time in the unlikely
cauldron of Bournemouth, a town where life begins at 60 and where
Lonnie Donegan is still number one in the charts. As The Times put it:
'To the sedate delight of the local inhabitants, Bournemouth carried
the flag of the Third Division into the last eight in the FA Cup.'

This Spurs team were a more accomplished outfit than their
predecessors (they finished runners-up in Division One in 1957) and
were 1-5 favourites for the tie. The previous week, they had scored
five goals in 23 minutes against Sunderland, form which prompted
the national press to predict that Bournemouth didn't have 'the
chance of a snowball in hell'.

But Bournemouth, managed by Freddie Cox, a protege of Spurs boss
Jimmy Anderson, were not just going to sit back and admire the fancy
footwork of Blanchflower and Co. Abandoning all niceties, they set
out to unnerve Spurs at every opportunity. These tactics had worked
at Wolves in the fourth round, as a result of which Cox received a
pre-match threat from 25 Tottenham Teddy Boys. The letter read:
'Cut out the commando stuff you used against the Wolves. Just try it
and we will do the same to you and your boys.' Cox wisely refrained
from showing it to the team and simply threw it in the bin.

Spurs were clearly not impressed by the antics of some of the
Bournemouth players, notably those of Ollie Norris, their fiery Irish
forward. Norris delighted in jumping up and down in front of the
Spurs players at throw-ins to distract them, none of the Tottenham men
showing the sense to step back a yard or two when taking the throw.

He also persisted in chasing keeper Ted Ditchburn around the penalty area whenever he tried to drop-kick clear. On one occasion, Ditchburn became so annoyed that he flatly refused to take a goal-kick.

To rub salt into the wound, it was Norris who opened the scoring after 13 minutes. Newsham passed to Cutler and the little winger beat Peter Baker before crossing for Norris to hook the ball past the despairing Ditchburn. Two minutes later, Spurs were level. Bobby Smith, who was closely marked throughout by his old Chelsea teammate Harry Hughes, sneaked the ball through to Welsh international Terry Medwin, whose rising drive left Bournemouth keeper Tommy Godwin clutching at air. Godwin then brought off a fine save to thwart Alf Stokes. Bournemouth's style of play, which at best could be described as direct, began to swamp Spurs. Defending in depth, they forced Tony Marchi and Danny Blanchflower to carry the ball

Nelson Stiffle fires Bournemouth's third goal, pursued in vain by Spurs full-back Mel Hopkins

well forward in order to start moves and when these broke down, long clearances opened the way for the fast-raiding Bournemouth forwards. On 35 minutes, Bournemouth regained the lead. Norris broke down the right and his deep cross was headed in by Stan Newsham. This goal provoked such uncharacteristic excitement that a fan sitting on a bench beneath the main stand leaped into the air and landed on the foot of linesman Mr C. Staite! The game was held up for a couple of minutes while the unfortunate official received treatment.

Then on the stroke of half-time, Brian Bedford had a header disallowed for offside. A third goal then would surely have sunk Tottenham but as it was, they were only spared for five minutes of the second half. Newsham delivered another long ball into the path of Nelson Stiffle who raced round Hopkins and cut in to beat Ditchburn with a fine shot from 15 yards. Spurs tried hard to get back into the game, bringing their wingers into the picture more, but Godwin was equal to everything they had to offer.

The result stirred the sleepy town that night. Ted Ray even made a joke about it on television and by the Monday, newsreels of the game were being shown at two local cinemas. No doubt 'The Jazz Singer' returned for the Tuesday...

Bournemouth & Boscombe Athletic: Godwin; Lyons, Woollard, Clayton, Hughes, Brown, Stiffle, Norris, Bedford, Newsham, Cutler.
Tottenham Hotspur: Ditchburn; Baker, Hopkins, Blanchflower, Ryden, Marchi, Medwin, Harmer, Smith, Stokes, Robb.
Referee: Mr J. Kelly (Chorley)
Attendance: 25,892

'I was confident we'd win after we got our second goal. We'll take on any Cup team at Dean Court in the future and beat them.'

Bournemouth's Ollie Norris
(they lost at home to Manchester United in the next round)

35

Northampton Town 3
Arsenal 1

4 January 1958

*O*llie Norris, the tormentor of Tottenham, quickly became yesterday's hero. The following season he put through his own goal as Bournemouth tumbled out of the Cup in the second round, 4-1 at Northampton. The reward for the Cobblers was a dream tie at home to Arsenal.

Plodding along sixth from bottom of Third Division (South), Northampton clearly needed something to lift their game for the occasion. The answer was a diet of sherry, eggs, glucose and orange juice, an interesting combination yet to feature on *Masterchef*.

It may have seemed to some that 'Flag-Kick' in the local *Chronicle and Echo* had been at the sherry from the way he confidently predicted a Northampton victory. He also reported that the BBC were showing highlights of the game in *Sports Special* and that 'Mr David Coleman, BBC Midland Region sports editor, was to do the television commentary from the camera vantage point.' One must hope Mr Coleman did not describe Town's alcoholic intake as 'a question of port'.

For the day of the match, it was announced that alcohol would also be available at the ground, from a marquee erected between the bowling club and the cricket scoreboard. Since the three-sided County Ground was not blessed with an abundance of seats, local farmers provided extra accommodation by supplying a number of carts!

Playing in unfamiliar old gold shirts (because of a colour clash), Arsenal appeared decidedly lack-lustre from the outset. They sat back and allowed Northampton to take control. The home defenders employed the simple tactic of kicking high and hard so that their

Arsenal keeper Jack Kelsey pulls off an acrobatic save to deny the eager Northampton forwards.

forwards were able to harry and hassle Bill Dodgin and his colleagues, all of whom seemed afraid of getting their shirts muddy. Perhaps they had to be back at the hire shop on Monday morning.

Only skipper Dave Bowen looked the part for Arsenal. The rest of the Gunners were firing blanks. Wingers Clapton and Nutt were virtually ignored; inside-forwards David Herd and Jimmy Bloomfield finished poorly; and centre-forward Groves was well held by Gale. When Groves did find himself faced with an open goal, he contrived to send the ball wildly into the crowd. *The Times* stated that Arsenal 'relied on skill that was never there.'

All three Northampton goals came from free-kicks, thereby exposing Arsenal's frailty in the air. The first came in the sixth minute, sixty seconds after Arsenal's Welsh international keeper Jack Kelsey had been hurt. He was obviously still feeling the effects of the injury when

Yeoman lofted a free-kick down the middle and young Bobby Tebbutt, a late replacement for food poisoning victim Alan Woan, went up among a sea of heads and saw his effort bounce gently into the net.

Although they scarcely deserved it, Arsenal were suddenly on level terms in the 30th minute. Elvy could only fist out Nutt's centre and Danny Clapton shot into the net. Then Northampton had an escape when Herd hit the post. Arsenal's spirit of adventure was short-lived, however, and Northampton resumed command in the second half. On the hour, a deflected free-kick from Gale was pursued to the by-line by English who pulled it back into the middle for Hawkings to side-foot the ball just inside the post. *The Times* noted that throughout this piece of action, Dodgin was rooted to the spot like a tree. The final nail in the Arsenal coffin was driven home in the 76th minute. Wills, who had earlier headed off the line with Kelsey beaten, hauled down Fowler. Mills's free-kick was sent into the box where it was met by Leek who shot through a forest of legs past the unsighted Kelsey.

The following year, Dave Bowen quit Arsenal to become manager of Northampton. In the style perfected by the Grand Old Duke of York, he proceeded to march Northampton up from the Fourth to the First Division and all the way back down again.

Northampton Town: Elvy; Collins, Patterson, Yeoman, Gale, Mills, English, Tebbutt, Hawkings, Leek, Fowler.
Arsenal: Kelsey; Wills, Evans, Holton, Dodgin, Bowen, Clapton, Herd, Groves, Bloomfield, Nutt.
Referee: Mr T.H. Cooper (Bolton)
Attendance: 21,344

'Of the old Arsenal greatness, there was no trace, not even a brave face or defiant rally when, nearing the end, the writing was on the wall. Arsenal, meek and mild, were pushed aside by a team boasting only speed and determination.'

The Times

36

Newcastle United 1
Scunthorpe United 3

25 January 1958

'Newcastle's trouble is that they have been losing matches all
season by small margins after having a fair share of the play. We
are confident of giving them a good game although most people
expect us to lose.'

Scunthorpe manager Ron Suart assessing his team's chances

N ewcastle were in decline. The glory team of the early Fifties was
slowly breaking up. Of the side which lifted the Cup in 1955,
only four turned out for the fourth-round tie with Third Division
(North) pace-setters Scunthorpe less than three years later. And some
of those were showing their age. At 31, left-winger Bobby Mitchell
was beginning to lose his sparkle.

After a shock defeat at Millwall the previous year, Newcastle were
keen to get back on the Wembley tail. They had started in the best
possible fashion with a 6-1 victory at Plymouth, Len White bagging
three and young George Eastham weighing in with a brace. But the
truth was that the reason for Newcastle's struggle in the First
Division was their abysmal home form – just three wins in 13 games.

Even without injured captain Bob Stokoe, Newcastle did not envisage
Scunthorpe barring their way to the twin towers. After all, the
Lincolnshire club, who had been in the League eight years, only just
managed to overcome local rivals Goole Town in an earlier round.
Consequently, Newcastle were keen to get the match played. An
army of 70 workers cleared tons of snow off the St James's Park pitch
and at 1.45pm on the Saturday, it was eventually passed fit for play,
much to the relief of the 3,000 travelling Scunthorpe fans.

Scunthorpe boss Ron Suart had watched Newcastle lose 2-1 at Chelsea the previous week and knew that they were far from invincible, particularly if Mitchell and right-half Jimmy Scoular could be subdued.

It soon became apparent that Newcastle were none too comfortable on a pitch which was a mixture of ice, water, mud and snow. Scoular and Mitchell were indeed shackled while Ronnie Simpson had a nightmare in the home goal and Alf McMichael was given the runaround by the speedy Marriott. Only Gordon Hughes, on the Newcastle right, looked threatening but he was slowed by a first-half injury. Whereas Scunthorpe opted to spread the play with long, diagonal passes, Newcastle were too slow in mounting attacks, allowing Scunthorpe time to get men behind the ball.

The writing was on the wall as early as the 25th minute when Ron Waldock surged through the mud to slide the ball under Simpson, only to see his effort disallowed for offside. Then, on the stroke of half-time, Scunthorpe took the lead. Marriott's corner was met by the leaping Jack Haigh and, although his header appeared to lack the necessary power, it eluded Simpson's belated dive.

Within five minutes of the restart, Newcastle were level. Mitchell made his one positive contribution to the match by winning a corner which he took himself. When it came over, centre-half Bill Paterson, a £22,000 signing from Doncaster, knocked it in. Scunthorpe full-back Jack Brownsword hooked it clear but the referee judged that it had just crossed the line. Newcastle's joy was short-lived, however. Five minutes later, Eric Davis, released by Plymouth the previous summer, beat Bill McKinney to head in Marshall's centre with Simpson hopelessly stranded.

Scunthorpe's cut-price heroes were in no mood to surrender their hard-won advantage. Three times Haigh had to receive attention but he insisted on continuing. With 15 minutes remaining, Davis put the seal on Scunthorpe's most famous triumph. Paterson missed Jones's cross and Davis capitalised on the error to shoot past Simpson. Davis celebrated the goal with a Maori war dance, an early variation on doing the lambada with the corner flag. There was certainly dancing in the streets of Scunthorpe that night – and that usually only happens when a big consignment of mushy peas hits town.

Newcastle United: Simpson; McKinney, McMichael, Scoular, Paterson, Franks, Hughes, Hale, White, Eastham, Mitchell.
Scunthorpe United: Hardwick; Sharpe, Brownsword, Marshall, Horstead, Bushby, Marriott, Waldock, Davis, Haigh, Jones.
Attendance: 39,407

37

Norwich City 3
Manchester United 0

10 January 1959

*O*nly two seasons previously, Norwich City had been forced to apply for re-election to the Football League after finishing bottom of Third Division (South). But manager Tom Parker (nobody could be expected to look after Elvis and the Canaries) had been replaced by Archie Macaulay, who soon brought about a revival in the club's fortunes.

In 1959, the Canaries were flying high in Division Three. Victories over Ilford and Swindon had also put them into the third round of the Cup where they were drawn against the previous year's beaten finalists, the post-Munich Manchester United. In East Anglia, it revived memories of City's earlier giant-killing feats of the Fifties, previous victims having included Liverpool (1951) and Arsenal (1954).

United were to finish second in the League in 1959 but on that greatest of levellers, the snow-covered pitch, they had no answer to a rampant Norwich team. Under the headline IT WAS GLORY, GLORY ALL THE WAY, the *Eastern Daily Press* declared: 'Charlton was but the palest of shadows of his great self of the Under-23 International, and only once did City have to indulge in the rankly unceremonious to stop him. If City had had the luck they deserved, or Gregg had not been in his best form, the rout must have been the most staggering of all the feats of giant-killing in Cup history.'

Macaulay had watched United at Chelsea and had drawn up a plan to exploit what weaknesses he saw. His trump card was 22-year-old centre-forward Terry Bly who gave United's young pivot Cope a most uncomfortable afternoon. Like most footballers, Bly was deeply superstitious. He always kissed his daughter Karen exactly three times before leaving for a game and told his wife to stay away from Carrow Road because her presence invariably seemed to bring him bad luck. Whether this decision caused mutiny in the Bly household is not known but Mrs. B's absence certainly seemed to work, for her husband totally outshone the nation's most expensive player, £45,000 Albert Quixall.

On an afternoon when 35 spectators were treated for the effects of the bitter cold, United struggled to keep their feet. Even so, they were the better side for the first 20 minutes but Bobby Charlton slipped over in a good position and Thurlow cleared an effort off the line. Then after 31 minutes, the Third Division team went ahead. Allcock made progress down the left and sent Brennan scurrying to the by-line. His pull-back was perfectly placed for Bly to run in and score.

The goal gave City tremendous heart. With Matt Crowe driving them on in midfield and skipper Ron Ashman, who was equalling the club record number of appearances, a tower of strength at the back, United hardly got a look-in. On a rare sortie, Dennis Viollet headed wide after Quixall had managed to outwit Ashman.

City pounded the visiting goal at the start of the second half. A Bly header shuddered the crossbar, in the process dislodging a layer of snow, Brennan struck the foot of a post and from the rebound, Allcock's shot was scrambled off the line. Finally, on 61 minutes, Norwich got the second goal their play deserved. Bly beat Carolan on the half-way line out on the left and headed down the wing. When the cross came over, Harry Gregg could only parry it to the waiting Crossan who nodded home despite the keeper's valiant attempt to redeem himself. And so it continued. Bly was denied by the diving Gregg, Allcock was narrowly off-target and Crossan had a 'goal' disallowed. But Norwich kept throwing men forward and were rewarded for their positive approach two minutes from time when Bly shrugged off Cope's challenge down the left and cut in to beat Gregg with an angled shot.

Norwich made it to the semi-finals that year before losing narrowly to Luton after a replay. The following season, they went out in the first round at Reading. Such is Cup football.

Norwich City: Nethercott; Thurlow, Ashman, McCrohan, Butler, Crowe, Crossan, Allcock, Bly, Hill, Brennan.
Manchester United: Gregg; Foulkes, Carolan, Goodwin, Cope, McGuinness, Bradley, Quixall, Viollet, Charlton, Scanlon.
Referee: Mr W. Clements (West Bromwich)
Attendance: 38,000

'They all laughed when I said we could beat Manchester United but I knew our men to be capable of winning. I planned two lines of defence. Right-half Roy McCrohan stayed back with the centre-half and full-back while Matt Crowe operated in front. As soon as a Norwich move broke down, inside-right Terry Allcock doubled back with Crowe. That way we were able to break up most of their moves before they started. I reckoned Billy Foulkes could be beaten so I told inside-left Jimmy Hill to stay on the wing with Bobby Brennan and that was where our goals came from. It worked to perfection. Terry Bly had all the room he needed in the middle and could have had half a dozen goals.'

Norwich manager Archie Macaulay

38

Worcester City 2
Liverpool 1

15 January 1959

'*W*orcester has never seen anything like it,' announced the city's *Evening Times* excitedly. 'Young boys and elderly gentlemen danced like dervishes side by side.' What could be the cause of such euphoria? The building of a new bus shelter on the Droitwich road? A personal appearance at the local Spar shop by Alma Cogan? No, it was the remarkable performance of Southern League Worcester City in removing such an illustrious name as Liverpool from the third round of the FA Cup.*

At the time, Liverpool occupied a place in the upper reaches of the Second Division. The Shankly era was just around the corner. They still had a fair side, built around former Scottish international goalkeeper Tommy Younger, but knew they could not afford to underestimate a Worcester team which had thrashed Millwall 5-2 in the previous round. Yet amazingly, they named the great Billy Liddell as 12th man.

Worcester manager Bill Thompson concocted the 'Thompson Plan' to cause the maximum amount of discomfort to Liverpool on the frozen St. George's Lane pitch. The plan was simple. The Worcester players concentrated on keeping the ball on the ground, making Liverpool's defenders twist and turn. Both Worcester goals came from appalling defensive blunders, the *Evening Times* remarking: 'The Liverpool rearguard were as nervous as old ladies on icy pavements.'

The first goal came after just nine minutes. Liverpool right-back Molyneux diverted a pass intended for Worcester winger Tommy Skuse out of the reach of the advancing Younger. Skuse and Liverpool centre-half White raced for the ball and, although White got there first, he merely succeeded in nudging the ball to Skuse who gleefully shot into the empty net. It was a great moment for Skuse who, at 18, was the youngest member of the team and who was so nervous that he was physically sick at half-time.

Driven on by their experienced captain Roy Paul, who had taken Manchester City to Wembley in 1955 and 1956, and his fellow wing-half Sammy Bryceland, Worcester continued to hold their own for the remainder of the first half, their defence rarely allowing the Liverpool forwards a sight of goal.

Liverpool began the second period with a renewed sense of purpose. Twentyman hit a post and Johnny Kirkwood in the home goal was called upon to make three fine saves: two from A'Court, the other from Morris. Worcester battled through this bad patch and then manager Thompson made a crucial tactical switch, getting centre-forward Knowles and outside-right Brown to swap positions. Brown's extra control in the middle and Knowles' fire and dash on the wing further served to unsettle the awkward Liverpool defenders. The move paid off in the 81st minute. Attempting to clear a square pass from Knowles, the unhappy White sliced the ball into his own net, high over Younger. A minute later, Melville was penalised for charging Bimpson, and Twentyman pulled one back from the spot. But Worcester held out comfortably and at the end, their players were chaired off the pitch by jubilant spectators. The city of Worcester was well and truly on the footballing map.

That day in 1959 undoubtedly saw the club's finest hour (and a half). In the fourth round, they lost 2-0 at home to Sheffield United and have only once since reached the third round. Their fortunes may have declined but they will always be remembered at Anfield.

Worcester City: Kirkwood; Wilcox, Potts, Bryceland, Melville, Paul, Brown, Follan, Knowles, Gosling, Skuse.
Liverpool: Younger; Molyneux, Moran, Wheeler, White, Twentyman, Morris, Melia, Bimpson, Harrower, A'Court.
Referee: Mr L. Tirebuck (Halifax)
Attendance: 15,111

'It was the biggest thrill I've ever had. There'll never be another goal like that one. Yet I wouldn't have scored if Liverpool centre-half White hadn't got a foot to the ball after Molyneux had diverted it past Younger. White and I ran for the ball together; he jabbed at it with his foot and simply teed it up for me. If he hadn't touched it, I'd never have reached it!'

Worcester goal-scorer Tommy Skuse

39

| Notts County | 0 |
| Bath City | 1 |

5 December 1959

'The City's performance was first-class but one must not forget the Bath supporters who travelled the 150 miles to Meadow Lane in order to spur their favourites to victory. They certainly did a grand job of work. From start to finish, they cheered, applauded, sounded their rattles and rang their bells. No one could ask for more.'

Bath Chronicle

*I*n terms of giant-killing, Southern Leaguers Bath City had always lived in the shadow of Somerset rivals Yeovil. Bath had nothing to compare with the scalp of Sunderland although they could point to wins over Crystal Palace in 1931, Southend in 1952 and Exeter in 1957.

But it was a 3-1 victory over Fourth Division Millwall in November 1959 which put the name of Bath City into the back page headlines. After a record-equalling unbeaten start to the League season of 19 games, the Lions had suffered their first defeat, at Notts County, just seven days before the Bath Cup tie. However Millwall had no answer to Bath's lively forwards and the home team were able to chalk up their 11th consecutive win. This set up a second-round trip to Meadow Lane.

Like Millwall, Notts County were chasing hard for promotion and had only failed to score at home once all season. The match certainly captured the imagination of the Nottingham public. For the first time in three years, all stand tickets were sold before kick-off, a 5,000 contingent from Bath swelling the attendance to the 25,000 mark, the biggest crowd ever to have watched the Southern League leaders.

What made Bath's triumph all the more praiseworthy was that their deadly marksman, club captain Charlie 'Cannonball' Fleming, pulled a muscle early on and was forced to operate in a much deeper role. Despite this setback, the non-Leaguers eagerly took the game to Notts.

After seeing a shot from Fleming drift wide, keeper Smith had to be at his most alert to turn a fierce drive from Thomas for a corner. Thomas had the beating of left-back Beeby and one of his runs led to Smith making a point-blank save from Wring. Notts' most dangerous forward was Horobin and three times in the opening period he came close to breaking the deadlock. First he headed a Roby cross just over the bar following a miskick by MacFarlane; then he sent a clever lob inches too high; and finally just before half-time sent Ian Black sprawling low to his left to save.

Then five minutes into the second half, Bath struck. Wring's cross was too deep for his fellow forwards but Thomas managed to retrieve the ball on the far side. Looking up, he wasn't exactly spoiled for choice until he spotted big Joe O'Neil lurking unmarked. O'Neil's shot was hard and true and Bath were ahead. It was a particularly timely strike since O'Neil was due to start a 14-day suspension two days later after being sent off in the Millwall tie.

County hit back but found the Bath defence, marshalled by Tony Book, later of Manchester City, in unyielding mood. Their best chance fell to Forrest but he was dispossessed by Black when about to shoot.

Bath's vociferous fans had plenty to shout about that night. Such was City's giant-killing reputation now that it was almost a surprise when they lost 1-0 at home to Second Division Brighton in the third round. Yeovil no longer had Somerset all to themselves.

40

Bradford City 3
Everton 0

9 January 1960

'Naturally I am very disappointed, but Bradford City played extremely well and fully deserved to win. Whoever they draw next can expect a hard game.'

Everton manager Johnny Carey

*I*t was 24 years since Bradford City had been drawn at home to a First Division side in the FA Cup. So the prospect of a visit from Everton whetted the appetites of the Yorkshire club's fans. And in front of a crowd of over 23,000, the club's second highest since the War, City did not disappoint.

By their standards, Everton were having a miserable season and had yet to win away from home. City, on the other hand, were enjoying a good run, unbeaten in 12 League and Cup ties, which had seen them steadily climb the Third Division table.

On the day, Everton were very much second best. With their forwards mastered by the resourceful City half-back line, in which Malcolm Devitt (playing his first Cup tie) was outstanding, Everton rarely threatened. The closest they came to scoring was when Stewart, in goal for the Cup-tied Downie, dropped the ball and breathed a sigh of relief as Laverick, the former Chelsea player, fired over the empty net.

The rest was all City. They had opened the scoring after only five minutes, David Jackson seizing on a loose ball to score from ten yards. They increased their lead seven minutes into the second half. As Alf Stokes, who had already scored six goals in City's Cup run, headed a Lawlor free-kick goalwards, Everton keeper Dunlop made the mistake of waiting for the ball to reach him. Showing a great turn of speed, City's Reid nipped in to take Dunlop by surprise and head into the unguarded net. By now, Everton were in total disarray. Webb hit the bar for City and Jackson, Stokes and Reid continued to create havoc in the Merseysiders' defence. The tie was finally put beyond Everton's reach in the 79th minute when Stokes sent a 30-yard piledriver into the roof of the net.

While City's League form slumped dramatically (in the end they only just avoided relegation to Division Four), they justified Johnny Carey's words in the Cup. After disposing of Bournemouth in the fourth round, it took Burnley, who three months later would be crowned First Division champions, to stop them. Even then, it needed a replay. It would be another 16 years before City again reached the fifth round of the Cup, but more of that later.

Bradford City: Stewart; Flockett, Mulholland, Devitt, Lawlor, Roberts, Webb, Jackson, Stokes, Reid, Boyle.
Everton: Dunlop; Bramwell, Parker, Jones, Labone, B. Harris, J. Harris, Wignall, Shackleton, Collins, Laverick.
Referee: Mr J.G. Williams (Nottingham)
Attendance: 23,550

41

9 January 1960

*M*idland Leaguers Peterborough United were the most formidable Cup side of the 1950s. There were more highlights than in Andy Townsend's hair at the 1994 World Cup as they took a string of League scalps – Torquay, Aldershot, Ipswich, Bradford Park Avenue, Lincoln, Shrewsbury and Walsall.

Ipswich, beaten 3-1 in 1955, certainly knew what to expect and manager Alf Ramsey was under no illusions about the task ahead in this third-round tie. Nevertheless, the Portman Road side were going well in the Second Division and were fresh from a six-goal blast against Leyton Orient. The Posh sat third in the Midland League, close behind North Shields and Ashington.

In a match played in a driving blizzard, Ramsey's urgency did not seem to communicate itself to his players. With the wind and snow at their backs, they had the opportunity to bury Peterborough in the opening quarter of an hour. The Posh defenders didn't even appear to be on first-name terms with each other but Ipswich seemed loath to capitalise on their opponents' distress. Town's best chance during this spell fell to Ray Crawford, but his fierce shot was safely clutched by keeper Daley.

Finally after 20 minutes, Ipswich stirred themselves. Ted Phillips's shot was cleared off the line by left-back Walker, only for Millward to latch on to the rebound and net from close range. Five minutes later, Crawford wasted another chance, flicking the ball well wide of an open goal after dribbling around Daley. Ipswich were made to pay dearly for these lapses when the visitors equalised three minutes from the interval, Rayner rounding off a slick move between Hails, McNamee and Smith. Almost immediately, Posh nearly went ahead but Hails's goal-bound effort was headed clear by Pickett.

Two minutes into the second half, Ipswich were back in front. Phillips took a neat pass from Leadbetter, hit the post, but netted the rebound. By now, Posh were virtually reduced to ten men, Walker operating at nothing more than a steady limp after twisting his right knee just before half-time. Undaunted, they pressed on and were rewarded with a second equaliser after 55 minutes, Emery finishing off a fine run by McNamee. Blinded by the blizzard, Ipswich visibly wilted in the face of a furious Peterborough onslaught, inspired by the tireless Smith. Hanging on grimly, the home side were three minutes from a replay when McNamee pushed the ball across their goal. Andy Nelson mis-kicked, allowing Emery to swivel and shoot left-footed past Bailey for another famous Peterborough victory.

It acquired even greater significance when Ipswich won the Second Division title the following season and the League Championship the year after that. Peterborough's reward was a place in Division Four for the 1960-61 season. Curiously, since they have acquired League status, Peterborough's FA Cup giant-killing deeds have become much less frequent with the notable exception of a 2-1 defeat of Arsenal in 1965.

Ipswich Town: Bailey; Carberry, Malcolm, Pickett, Nelson, Elsworthy, Owen, Millward, Crawford, Phillips, Leadbetter.
Peterborough United: Daley; Stafford, Walker, Banham, Rigby, Chadwick, Hails, Emery, Rayner, Smith, McNamee.
Referee: Mr J.W. Hunt (Portsmouth)
Attendance: 26,000

'**The little ground was suddenly full of bobbing Peterborough heads, a youth with a ginger crew cut became hysterical, and three schoolboys rushed on to the pitch before the game was allowed to wind out to the finish.**'

The Times reporting 'crowd disturbances'
following Peterborough's winning goal

42

Chelsea 1
Crewe Alexandra 2

7 January 1961

F *or the players of Crewe Alexandra, the streets of London were paved with misery. On their previous FA Cup visit to the capital, eleven months earlier, they had been routed 13-2 by Spurs. It was an experience they were not anxious to repeat. So it was with some trepidation that the Fourth Division outfit journeyed to Chelsea for a third-round tie, their fears founded on the Londoners' all-star forward line of Peter Brabrook, Jimmy Greaves, Ron Tindall, Bobby Tambling and Frank Blunstone. There was also a young right-half called Terry Venables. I wonder whatever happened to him?*

Yet Crewe's cause was by no means hopeless. Chelsea had lost their last two First Division games 6-0 at Manchester United and 6-1 at Wolves and had not been immune to the odd dose of giant-killing, witness a 4-1 exit at Darlington in 1958. And there was a suggestion that sixth-in-the-table Crewe had conquered their London phobia that season, having remained undefeated there, albeit at less exalted venues such as Crystal Palace and Millwall.

A contingent of 6,000 Crewe supporters travelled south for the Chelsea game. Crewe-born Frank Blunstone, son of a railway ticket collector, and who had left Alexandra eight years previously for a princely £8,000, was made Chelsea captain for the day against his old club. It was not an occasion which he and his team-mates would wish to remember.

Crewe boss Jimmy McGuigan felt that if they could shut out Greaves, his boys were in with a chance. A lot of managers came to that conclusion, before and after 1961, but putting the idea into practice was a different matter. Fortunately for Crewe, they had two defensive giants on the day in goalkeeper Brian Williamson and centre-half Eric Barnes. As a result, Greaves was rendered anonymous. It was enough to make a chap turn to drink.

The visitors struck as early as the fifth minute. Their playmaker Terry Tighe delivered a superb pass out to Shepherd. The ball was moved on to Foster whose cross eluded Peter Bonetti for Stark to score. Crewe were not finished yet. In the 27th minute, Tighe, receiving the ball on the right, fed Stark and his centre was firmly headed in by Barry Wheatley.

The shaken Chelsea fans saw a glimmer of hope four minutes later when Blunstone raced through to score with an unstoppable drive.

Barry Wheatley heads Crewe's second goal past the despairing Peter Bonetti. The 'Cat' is left looking like Bagpuss.

The second half was nearly all Chelsea. Greaves, given a rare sniff of goal, hit the post and could only watch helplessly as the ball rolled along the line before being hoofed away. Crewe also hacked two other efforts off the line as their goal led a charmed life. Their sole reply was a shot from Stark which beat Bonetti but clipped the post.

Somehow Crewe survived and their players and fans danced with delight at the final whistle, oblivious to the sight of Greaves walking off alone, dejected, his shirt held to his face.

The *Crewe Chronicle* greeted the wondrous win with the headline 'EVERY MAN IN A RED SHIRT WAS A HERO'. When the TV and Press cameras turned up for the fourth-round draw, club secretary Tom Garnett remarked: 'Gresty Road was like Hollywood.' With no sign of Elizabeth Taylor using the outside toilet, it is just possible that this was something of an exaggeration.

The Crewe players wanted to meet Spurs again in the next round (their manager was not so sure) and, amazingly, their dreams were realised. The outcome was the same, however, although this time by the more respectable score of 5-1. The ghost had been partly exorcised.

Chelsea: Bonetti; P.Sillett, Harris, Venables, Evans, Anderton, Brabrook, Greaves, Tindall, Tambling, Blunstone.
Crewe Alexandra: Williamson; McGill, Campbell, Keery, Barnes, Shepherd, Stark, Tighe, Foster, Wheatley, M.Jones.
Referee: Mr R.E. Smith (Newport)
Attendance: 32,574

'Not even Greaves, shadowed all afternoon, could rescue the losers against a firmly-organised, enthusiastic defence which rose to great heights.'

The Times

43

25 November 1961

'Morecambe, town of glittering lights, haven't any to sparkle
brighter than the 11 footballers who produced another page of club
history by putting them into the third round of the Cup for the first
time. They illuminated Sealand Road with a brand of football that
made Chester look like a bunch of non-Leaguers.'

The People

*F*ootball reporters are often accused of never having been at the
match. Judging by the comments of the People reporter, one can
only assume he has never been to Morecambe. Glittering lights? He
must have meant the flashing belisha beacons. To make his glowing
prose all the more unlikely, it appeared in the same week that the
local Morecambe paper carried the front-page headline: 'TOWN IS IN
A HELL OF A MESS', referring to complaints about the resort's
untidiness.

The local football club had hitherto done little to enhance the town's
image. In their 60-year existence, the Lancashire Combination team
had reached the first round proper of the FA Cup on just three
occasions. Each time they had lost. The fourth was 1961 and a
stunning 2-1 victory over South Shields set them up for a day out at
Chester in round two.

Floundering near the foot of the Fourth Division in this the season in
which Accrington Stanley resigned from the League, Chester were
further hit when centre-half Kennedy failed a late fitness test, thereby
causing a hasty reshuffle. Nevertheless, their ranks did include
rugged half-back Doug Hennin who had won a Cup winners' medal

with Bolton three years earlier. Hennin was not renowned for exchanging pleasantries with opposing forwards.

What turned out to be the only goal of the game came in the first minute – and a bizarre affair it was too, reminiscent of a classic Keystone Cops adventure. As Morecambe went straight on to the offensive, centre-forward Borrowdale beat Gill, only to be nudged from behind and lose possession. No foul was given but Chester goalkeeper Hardie, who had run out to clear, succeeded in slicing his kick horribly. It looped up in the air towards Morecambe winger Howarth who headed goalwards. By now, Chester full-back Hughes had positioned himself on the line but he too made a botch of things, simply nodding the ball straight back to Howarth who squeezed the ball home at the second attempt. On such moments is Cup glory won and lost.

Morecambe continued to make the running, with Evans embarking on a series of mazy runs, often beating three men at a time. Just before the break, Morecambe had loud penalty appeals rejected when Whitehead appeared to be knocked off the ball in the act of shooting. With Dunn marshalling the visitors' defence, Udall's goal was rarely threatened. Apart from a dash out to block Cartlidge after an error by Cubbage, the keeper's only moment of anxiety was in the closing minutes when Hennin had a headed 'goal' disallowed for an infringement. Hennin's reaction was probably not printable. The Chester fans were not impressed either and, while Morecambe basked in their glory, home supporters staged an after-match demonstration outside the Sealand Road boardroom.

It is one of the tragic ironies of FA Cup history that what was until then the most important moment in Morecambe Football Club's life was missed by all but a handful of its supporters. And it was all down to our old friends, British Railways. For the train taking 700 Morecambe fans to the match arrived the obligatory 13 minutes late at Chester and the buses hired to take them from the station to the ground were held up in heavy traffic. As a result, none of the supporters who travelled by train saw the winning goal. Some things never change...

Chester: Hardie; Hughes, Donaldson, Morris, Gill, Hennin, Fitzgerald, White, Davies, Cartlidge, Jones.
Morecambe: Udall; Cubbage, Richardson, Dunn, Scott, Keen, Fawcett, Evans, Borrowdale, Whitehead, Howarth.
Referee: Mr H. Webb (Leeds)
Attendance: 7,965

44

Coventry City 1
King's Lynn 2

25 November 1961

If ever a club needed a Cup run, it was King's Lynn. £1,500 in debt and one off the foot of the Southern League, the Norfolk part-timers had already beaten Chelmsford City and now found Third Division Coventry standing between them and a possible big pay day with one of the glamour clubs in the third round.

Coventry hadn't lost to a non-League team since Midland League Scunthorpe put them out of the 1935-36 competition, but their performance here suggested that they were anxious to make up for lost time. They were even gifted a goal start in the 28th minute. The Linnets' Dunn challenged City inside-forward Hill for a loose ball. 'Keeper Manning came out to collect but the ball squirted across goal out of his reach. Hindle kicked away but his clearance struck the returning Manning and rebounded into the net.

City failed to profit from this comedy of errors and five minutes later, the scores were level. The visitors had already missed four good chances when centre-forward Ray Dixon chipped the ball over Bennett's head and Mick Johnson, a last-minute replacement for 'flu victim Bobby Brennan, was able to score with Lightening in the

Coventry goal singularly failing to live up to his name. Three minutes later, Bacon crossed for Mick Wright to head in off the underside of the bar and King's Lynn were in the lead.

And that was how it stayed. Bobby Lumley schemed and foraged, launching countless King's Lynn attacks; Ray Dixon, despite an early knee injury, gave George Curtis a harrowing time; and keeper Mick Manning remained in more danger from his own defenders than the Coventry forwards. In a desperate, late City flourish, Mike Dixon fired a yard over the bar.

Victorious manager Len Richley put the shock result down to 'absolute teamwork', while the *Lynn News and Advertiser* proclaimed: 'It was thoroughly deserved and so undeniably convincing that everyone who made the long trip for the game felt proud to be a Linnet.' The final statement suggests that the reporter was on something stronger than Spangles.

King's Lynn got their third-round payday from a 4-0 defeat at Goodison Park while, four days after this debacle, Coventry sacked manager Billy Frith. His replacement was someone called Jimmy Hill. City fans thought things could never get any worse in the Cup. But then many had probably never even heard of Sutton United…

Coventry City: Lightening; Bennett, Kletzenbauer, Nicholas, Curtis, Austin, P. Hill, Hewitt, M. Dixon, B. Hill, Imlach.
King's Lynn: Manning; Mackey, Wilson, Dunn, Hindle, Sanchez, Bacon, Lumley, R. Dixon, Johnson, Wright.
Attendance: 12,080

'In probably the most grim page in City's modern history, a team of part-timers inscribed their indelible mark by sweeping their Third Division opponents out of the FA Cup and leaving shocked and stunned City fans to wonder how a League side gave such puny and deplorably inept resistance.'

Coventry Evening Telegraph, 1961

45

Carlisle United 0
Gravesend & Northfleet United 1

29 January 1963

'I thought I couldn't get it. Then, in a flash, I knew I could and just managed to get my boot to the ball at the last second before it crossed the line.'

Gravesend & Northfleet's match-saver Harry McDonald

Since merging with Northfleet United in 1946, Gravesend had never progressed beyond the first round proper of the Cup. But in 1962-63, the North Kent town which is best known for absolutely nothing embarked on an epic voyage of discovery. First, Exeter were defeated 3-2, then Wycombe Wanderers 3-1 to earn the Southern Leaguers something they could probably have done without – namely a 600-mile round-trip to that great northern outpost of Carlisle. What made the prospect even less palatable was that bad weather forced the tie to be postponed no fewer than six times. By the time they got round to playing, the teams knew that awaiting the winners was a more appetising home fourth-round tie with Sunderland.

Carlisle were battling against relegation to Division Four but Gravesend were not exactly world-beaters either, having mustered just one away win all season. Any pre-match plans Gravesend may have entertained were scuppered when Carlisle's left-winger Sammy Taylor was taken ill three hours before the game eventually took place, thus necessitating a wholesale reshuffle of the home attack.

Carlisle made all of the early running, scything through the Gravesend defence at will. But time and again, they were denied by the heroics of Gravesend's second-choice keeper Peter Reader. It was not until the 20th minute that Gravesend launched their first serious attack and with it they scored what was to prove the decisive goal. With feet movement reminiscent of driving the Flintstones' car, Brian Skingley skipped through the mud in the middle of the pitch and laid a ball on to Bobby Cameron. He in turn slipped the ball to the lanky Tony Sitford who was screaming for a pass. From just outside the box, Sitford exploded a drive which thudded into the stanchion and rebounded some 30 yards back onto the pitch before coming to rest in a puddle. The first Carlisle keeper Joe Dean saw of it was on its way out.

Winger Williams nearly increased Gravesend's advantage but his close-range shot stuck in the mud two feet from the goal-line with Dean beaten.

Carlisle slowly began to assume control but, with Tony Newcombe blotting out the lively Joe Livingstone, their chances were restricted. Reg Davies squandered two good openings in the first half but just before the break, was denied by an acrobatic save from Reader. Davies let fly and saw his shot take a wicked deflection off Gravesend defender Ernie Walley. Somehow Reader reacted to palm the ball to safety. And when Reader was beaten by Ron Thompson, Harry McDonald popped up from nowhere to make a dramatic goal-line clearance.

In a desperate final Carlisle assault, Dagger had a last-minute effort disallowed for offside (shades of the Cheltenham tie) and there was still time for Dave Oliphant to send a 35-yard drive screaming just wide of the post.

As Gravesend celebrated, club secretary George Fooks revealed that he had been so confident of victory that he had Sunderland's ticket quota of 3,300 printed before the game so that he could take them with him to Brunton Park. At the end, he proceeded to hand them over to stunned Sunderland officials.

Gravesend went on to hold Sunderland 1-1 before losing the replay 5-2. It had been a gallant effort. As the *Gravesend Reporter* wrote, previewing the Sunderland tie: 'Monday night in Northfleet will be a night to remember!' Well, I suppose there's a first-time for everything.

46

Newport County 3
Sheffield Wednesday 2

4 January 1964

'We are doing reasonably well in the First Division, so I do not think we shall worry unduly about meeting Newport. I know it never does to underestimate opponents but surely we cannot be anything other than confident of winning.'

Sheffield Wednesday manager Vic Buckingham,
previewing the third-round tie with Newport

*D*escribed as the most exciting game ever seen at Somerton Park (which admittedly is like talking about the most exciting edition of The Money Programme), this was the Cup-tie from which nobody outside Newport expected anything other than a comfortable Wednesday win. For although they were without England goalkeeper Ron Springett and talented inside-forward John Fantham, Wednesday were one of the form teams in the First Division (they eventually finished sixth). Meanwhile, Newport, as was their wont, were ambling along in the lower reaches of the Fourth Division. In truth, even the locals didn't give Newport much of a chance.

Fortunately, the players were more optimistic. Home victories over Hereford and Watford in the earlier rounds had boosted confidence, but they were all too aware of the vigilance required to shackle the Wednesday wingers, Alan Finney and former England international Ted Holliday. As it was, home full-backs Bird and Walters never allowed the speed and trickery of Finney and Holliday to overwhelm them while the eager Newport forwards responded to the probing of wing-halves John Rowland and Len Hill, the latter displaying some particularly delightful touches.

What made County's display all the more creditable was that they had to come from behind. On 20 minutes, Newport keeper Len Weare needlessly parried a shot from Dobson which was going wide. It dropped to the feet of Holliday who swept home. But it was the second-half action which really raised the roof at Somerton Park, something which a sudden gust of wind had also been known to do.

Three minutes after the break, the crowd swarmed onto the pitch to greet Newport's equaliser. Skipper Joe Bonson beat Wednesday full-back Hill to the ball to head home Webster's corner. In the 56th minute, Finney restored Wednesday's advantage with a brilliant solo effort but on 69 minutes, County hit back again, Bonson scoring his second after Maclaren had driven a clearance straight to him. Two minutes later, the crowd were over the walls again. County winger Smith cut in from the left, beat Maclaren, and Ralph Hunt steamed in to force the ball over the line. The pitch invasions brought three minutes of injury time, during which Weare atoned for his earlier mistake with a flying save from Holliday.

As the celebrations began, match-winner Joe Bonson beamed: 'Before the match I told the lads that they were as good as the Wednesday and they proved it.' In his post-match summing-up, the Mayor of Newport chose to ignore the various merits of deep-lying centre-forwards and overlapping full-backs, preferring to concentrate on the crowd's lusty singing of 'Cwm Rhondda'. Well, he was Welsh.

47

Newcastle United 1
Bedford Town 2

4 January 1964

*N*ewport's success was rather overshadowed by events a few
hundred miles away on that same January afternoon. For
Southern League Bedford, comprising two full-timers, three builders,
three engineers, two decorators and a draughtsman, created an
almighty upset by conquering Second Division Newcastle, whose
team had cost over £250,000 to assemble, at their St James's Park
fortress.

Bedford, who back in 1956 had held Arsenal to a draw at Highbury
before losing the replay in extra-time, had been left in limbo after
defeating Chelmsford in the second round of this year's competition.
Manager Reg Smith had suddenly departed for South Africa, leaving
club stalwart Tim Kelly to hold the reins in a caretaker capacity. He
was still in charge by the time the Newcastle tie came around
although Bedford were awaiting Basil Hayward's release from Yeovil.

The Eagles of Bedford (they played at The Eyrie) were 1,000 to 1
outsiders for the FA Cup. But, armed with their lucky mascot, a china
black cat, Kelly's heroes set out to humiliate Newcastle. That cat was
not their only lucky omen. The match referee, Mr Crawford, had been
in charge of Kettering's surprise win at Millwall two months earlier.
And, little did they know it, but they had an even better talisman in

the shape of goalkeeper Jock Wallace. For three years later, Wallace was to keep goal for Berwick Rangers in their memorable Scottish Cup triumph over Glasgow Rangers. Wallace was the only Bedford player with experience of St James's Park – he had played there for a Blackpool junior XI when he was 15.

Bedford almost got off to a disastrous start. David Coney's back pass beat Wallace and was trickling towards the empty net when Mike Collins materialised to scoop the ball off the line. It produced the first of Newcastle's 16 corners to Bedford's two.

Slowly, Bedford began to settle down with Bill Goundry running midfield and John Fahy proving a handful to Newcastle centre-half John McGrath. Fahy, whose £3,000 move to Oxford United was on hold until the end of the Cup run, had already seen a 21st-minute shot well saved when he struck the opening blow eight minutes later. David Lovell's cross from the right landed perfectly for Fahy to head a textbook goal. Newcastle became increasingly jittery at the back and three minutes before the break, a move between David Sturrock, Ron Heckman and Goundry produced a low, hard cross which cannoned off United's Bill McKinney and into the net.

The Eagles were well on top in the second half with Marshall making two fine saves to deny former Leyton Orient, Millwall and Palace forward Heckman. Newcastle's only response was a 65th-minute effort from Stan Anderson which brought a great stop from Wallace. It all became too much for some home supporters who proceeded to hurl straw onto the pitch! Play was held up for several minutes while the debris was cleared and during the time added on for the stoppage, Anderson's cracking 30-yarder pulled one back for United.

Bedford were worthy winners, leaving Newcastle director Stan Seymour to label United's performance as 'puerile'. Manager Joe Harvey added solemnly: 'This was one of our worst displays.' After winning at Newcastle, Bedford must have fancied their chances when the fourth round gave them a home draw with Fourth Division Carlisle. Such are the vagaries of football that Bedford crumbled 3-0.

'I knew I had a tough job in holding Barrie Thomas. I played against him twice when I was with Luton and he played for Scunthorpe. I was determined that if he was to get by me, it would be over my dead body. As for the game, Newcastle lost their composure after we got our second goal.'

Bedford man-of-the-match Mike Collins

48

Aldershot 2
Aston Villa 1

8 January 1964

Renowned Cup fighters Aston Villa must have thought that a third-round tie with Fourth Division Aldershot at Villa Park would be little more than a formality. Yet against all the odds, the Hampshire team scrambled a goalless draw. Joe Mercer's Villa were still hot favourites for the replay four days later, particularly since the huge tree behind one goal at the Recreation Ground had a reputation for being more mobile than the Aldershot forwards. But Villa were undone by two fluke goals in the last 20 minutes.

The first half was a non-event. Defences dominated, the only chances falling to Villa's Burrows and Aldershot's Fogg, both of whom shot over from good positions. Crowe and Tindall worked hard for Villa but *The Times* reported that the Aldershot players 'stuck like leeches, and if somehow the opponent slipped from their grasp, they were on him again in a flash, never giving up until the ball was dead.' Villa began by playing Fourth Division football, clearing their lines with a hefty boot upfield, before eventually adopting a short-passing game which became entangled in a web of over-elaboration.

Aldershot were a much more potent force in the second half, proving a constant threat from set pieces. Earlier, they hadn't looked capable of crossing a pools coupon but in the first three minutes alone, they went close from three free-kicks and a corner. However after 69 minutes, the game was still scoreless. Then Aldershot were awarded a free-kick out near the right touchline, some seven yards from the corner flag. Jim Towers stood over the ball, shaped as if he was leaving it to a team-mate but then whipped over a cross. Villa keeper Sims saw it coming, only to make a mess of his dive and see the ball curve into the net over his outstretched hands.

The blunder caused Villa to fall apart. Chris Palethorpe hit a post, Burton shot just wide and then Palethorpe curled a 75th-minute corner straight into the net with Sims again badly at fault. Tony Hateley did manage to bundle one in with a minute left but it was too late to save their skins.

For the previous five years, Villa had been knocked out by the eventual Cup winners. The saying was: 'The team who beats Villa wins the Cup.' *The Times* mused: 'Who is to deny Aldershot their right to such dreams?' The answer was Swindon in the next round.

Aldershot: Jones; Devereux, Renwick, Smith, Henry, Mulgrew, Palethorpe, Priscott, Fogg, Towers, Burton.
Aston Villa: Sims; Wright, Aitken, Crowe, Sleeuwenhoek, Deakin, MacEwan, Ewing, Hateley, Tindall, Burrows.
Referee: Mr G.W. Davis (Romford)
Attendance: 13,566

49

Oxford United 3
Blackburn Rovers 1

15 February 1964

*H*eadington United were noted giant-killers of the Fifties, numbering Millwall and Stockport among their victims. In 1960, they changed their name to Oxford United and two years later, joined the Football League. And in only their second season as League members, they maintained the club's fine Cup tradition by reaching the quarter-finals of the FA Cup, the first Fourth Division side to do so. Folkestone, Kettering, Chesterfield and Brentford had all been swept aside but the big test would be the fifth-round visit of Blackburn Rovers to the Manor Ground.

With defensive stalwarts in Ronnie Clayton, 35 caps for England, and Mike England of Wales, the probing of silky-skilled inside-forward Bryan Douglas and the cutting edge of international colleague Fred Pickering, Blackburn were an extremely useful side. Although missing right-back Keith Newton, injured in an England training session, they were second in Division One at the time. They eventually finished seventh in the League that season, 79 places above Oxford. But such statistics are irrelevant when it comes to the Cup.

Oxford had some seasoned campaigners of their own. Centre-half Maurice Kyle was making his 250th first-team appearance and inside-left Tony Jones was recalled to play his 200th game for the club. Their driving force was their young captain, barrel-chested right-half Ron Atkinson, affectionately known as 'The Tank'. As he rolled forward down the Manor Ground slope, threatening to crush anything in his path, it has to be said there was a certain similarity. These qualities prompted United manager Arthur Turner to declare before the match: 'I can promise Blackburn it will not be a pushover. We may have a few surprises for them.'

Local bookmaker Jim Bailey was offering United a week at Worthing if they won. No doubt it was two weeks if they lost. Many Blackburn fans had left Lancashire at 11.30pm on the Friday night. Those who had gone straight to the Manor Ground at the crack of dawn promptly headed back into the city. The *Oxford Mail* observed: 'They challenged the odd passer-by, swinging their rattles and bells and calling a cheery "Good morning" through the occasional letter-box. As nine o'clock approached, a knot gathered outside Woolworth's and chanted to the passengers disembarking from city buses.' It was arguably less taxing than waiting to be served at the Pick 'n' Mix counter.

Come the afternoon and Oxford's quaint little ground was bursting at the seams. At regular intervals throughout the match, the crowd spilled over the touchlines, unable to find accommodation under United's array of covering, some of which would not have looked out of place as school bicycle sheds.

It soon became apparent that Blackburn had woefully underestimated their opponents. Oxford chased everything while Blackburn,

Oxford's Tony Jones (second from right) scores United's first goal against Blackburn.

displaying a streak of arrogance, were content to rely on their superior skills. Against Oxford's ferocious tackling, it was not enough. Kyle kept Pickering quiet and Douglas was hustled out of the game, taking a fearful battering in the process.

The hero of the day was the recalled Jones. Else in the Blackburn goal had already been forced to tip over a shot from Beavon when he found himself picking the ball out of the net in the 14th minute. Shuker sent Longbottom away down the right. The fast, low cross was missed by Calder but Jones made no mistake, stabbing home from close range. Early in the second half, McEvoy spurned a chance to equalise by slicing his shot and Oxford quickly punished the lapse. A fine deep cross from Shuker found Calder's head at the far post. He laid it back for Jones to drive past Else. Ferguson gave Rovers a glimmer of hope in the 67th minute, shooting through a crowd of players, but just before the finish, with a number of spectators on the pitch, Calder settled the outcome, tapping in the third from Quartermain's low cross.

Jones kept up his scoring run when United entertained another Lancashire side, Preston, in the quarter-finals a fortnight later. His goal could not prevent Preston going through 2-1, but by then the name of Oxford United had already made its mark on the FA Cup.

Oxford United: Fearnley; Beavon, Quartermain, R. Atkinson, Kyle, Shuker, Knight, Longbottom, Calder, Jones, Harrington.
Blackburn Rovers: Else; Bray, Joyce, Clayton, England, McGrath, Ferguson, McEvoy, Pickering, Douglas, Harrison.
Referee: Mr G. McCabe (Sheffield)
Attendance: 21,000

'Nothing perhaps summed up the delight and surprise of this memorable victory so well as the sight of Atkinson, the young Oxford captain, being carried shoulder high from a field black with people as tears rolled down his grimy, smiling face.'

The Times reporting the unforgettable occasion when a crowd of 21,000 were able to lift Ron Atkinson

50

Millwall 2
Fulham 0

11 January 1965

'The plan was to exploit George Cohen and Bobby Robson. I knew both liked to get forward as often as possible. Cohen loved using his speed to get in crosses but I reckoned that for every decent cross he managed to get into the box, nine others would end up amongst the folk behind the goal. So we planned to allow Cohen space to get forward as often as possible, keep Robson marked on his deep runs and, once they were committed, play the ball into the gaps they left behind.'

Millwall manager Billy Gray

*F*ew *clubs have been the butt of so many jokes as Fulham. When Tommy Trinder was chairman, he almost built his act around them. Year after year in the Sixties, they had the last laugh, somehow managing to cheat relegation from the First Division. Their exploits earned them the tag of the Houdinis of football.*

Fulham's team was moulded around four key players – acrobatic goalkeeper Tony Macedo, a man who would sign autographs with a full-length dive, former England stars Johnny Haynes and Bobby Robson and the current international right-back, George Cohen. It may have looked a daunting line-up to most Fourth Division managers but not to Millwall boss Billy Gray. A member of Nottingham Forest's 1959 Cup winning team, Gray admitted that he probably knew more about plotting the downfall of First Division opposition than the likes of Hartlepools, Barrow and Southport. So he produced his master-plan and had his players perfecting it in the week prior to the third-round tie at Craven Cottage.

Millwall had opened that year's Cup campaign by gaining revenge for the previous season's ignominious defeat at the hands of Kettering and, although their League form had dipped around Christmas, the Lions had unearthed a promising young goalkeeper in Alex Stepney, signed from Tooting & Mitcham. From 3-1 down, Millwall fought back to snatch a 3-3 draw and achieve the replay that no club relished – a trip to The Den.

With only 5,000 inside, The Den could sound like a cauldron, so with over 30,000 packed in that Monday night the noise was deafening. Fulham included a young inside-forward by the name of Rodney Marsh and opened brightly, Stepney plunging to stop a 20-yarder from Haynes in the tenth minute. Shortly afterwards, Stratton's curling shot beat Stepney but grazed the far post. Urged on by the crowd, Millwall hit back. Hughie Curran twice headed just too high and then winger Barry Rowan, a £300 signing from Dover, outpaced Jim Langley and saw his shot skim the bar. However the fates seemed to be conspiring against Millwall when their influential wing-half Dave Harper had to be helped off in the 39th minute after sustaining rib and hip injuries. Following heat treatment and three pain-killing tablets, Harper amazingly returned for the second half (there was no substitute ruling in those days) as an emergency centre-forward. He could barely walk let alone run.

For 67 minutes, Fulham resisted the tidal wave of Millwall attacks, only to fall behind in sensational, if somewhat unfortunate, fashion. Rowan mis-hit his shot completely but who should it fall to but the hobbling Harper who defied the pain barrier to lash the ball past Macedo from six yards. Fulham threw everyone forward in search of an equaliser but, with just a few minutes remaining, the ball again broke to the heroic Harper. Conjuring up a last ounce of strength, he managed to push the ball through to Rowan whose shot beat Macedo to ensure that there wouldn't be too much laughter in the Fulham boardroom that night. After the game, a frustrated Robson declared: 'It was thoroughbreds against donkeys.' To which Gray replied: 'You're right. The donkeys had two tries…and still lost!'

51

Luton Town 0
Corby Town 1

7 December 1965

In 1959, First Division Luton Town had marched out at Wembley to face Nottingham Forest in the Cup Final. Six years later, they were in the Fourth Division. An indication of their decline was their humiliation at the hands of Southern Leaguers Corby Town, a club whose interest in the Cup has always lasted about as long as the British challenge at Wimbledon.

After taking two attempts to dispose of Romford in the first round, Luton scrambled a 2-2 draw at Corby thanks to a controversial penalty five minutes from time. If they thought they had done the hard part, they were sorely mistaken. Still smarting from the penalty incident, Corby were determined to finish the job at Kenilworth Road.

The Corby manager, Tommy Hadden, was one of those loyal club servants so rife in non-League football. He had been player, trainer and team coach (until he broke down on the way to a match at Hastings) but this was his greatest night with The Steelmen. He knew that Luton's danger man was centre-forward John O'Rourke and detailed Tony Needham to get closer to him than most couples do on a first date. It took a few minutes for the tactic to work, time in which O'Rourke wasted away two chances which would later prove costly.

121

After their nervous opening, Corby settled down to take command. They forced four corners in quick succession and saw George Jagger drive narrowly wide. Then in the 33rd minute came what turned out to be the winning goal. Charlie McGlinchey, back in the team following a long spell in the reserves, collected the ball in his own half and sent skipper Alex Stenhouse away down the right wing. Reaching the by-line, Stenhouse pulled the ball back for Maurice Goodall to run in and beat Tinsley. For Goodall, it made up for the chances he had missed in the first game.

Luton became increasingly frustrated as the match wore on and Corby could have increased their lead. Garden beat Tinsley but was unable to force the ball over the line; McGlinchey had a header cleared off the line by Thomson; and Tinsley smothered a shot from Goodall. Corby almost lived to regret their extravagance when, in the very last minute, O'Rourke escaped Needham's attentions to send in a flashing header which skimmed the bar.

But Corby were able to savour their moment of glory, reaching the third round for the only time in their history. It was not a pleasant experience. They crashed 6-0 at Plymouth.

Luton Town: Tinsley; Thomson, Edwards, Reid, Woods, Moore, Harber, Read, O'Rourke, Gibson, Whittaker.
Corby Town: Alexander; Whittaker, Pollard, Riley, Needham, Armour, McGlinchey, Stenhouse, Goodall, Garden, Jagger.
Referee: Mr R.V. Spittle (Great Yarmouth)
Attendance: 13,000

'I am proud of all the lads but I heaved a sigh of relief when that header from O'Rourke went over the bar just before the final whistle. After the game, Maurice Goodall was holding up the boot that brought the goal and he was so thrilled, he was shaking like a leaf.'

Corby manager Tommy Hadden

52

Hull City 2
Nottingham Forest 0

12 February 1966

'I think we will win first time. We have got a better side now than when Forest won the Cup in 1959.'

A Nottingham Forest fan's confident prediction before the Cup tie at Hull

*U*nder Johnny Carey, Nottingham Forest were a useful side in the 1960s. They finished fifth in the First Division in 1965 and were runners-up in 1967. By contrast, their League form of 1965-66 was less satisfactory and they spent most of the season in the bottom half of the table.

After winning 2-1 away to fellow First Division strugglers Northampton in the third round, Forest faced a stiff test at Third Division leaders Hull whose striking quartet of Ken Wagstaff, Chris Chilton, Ken Houghton and Ian Butler was, on its day, the equal of any in the land. The burly Wagstaff, in particular, was a folk hero on Humberside where such reverence is usually reserved for cod. Actor and City fan Tom Courtenay was such a devotee that he actually named his dog Wagstaff!

So Forest were under no illusions about the task ahead, especially since they had been knocked out of the competition by a side from a lower division in each of the previous three seasons – namely Southampton, Preston and Crystal Palace. To add to the sense of foreboding in the Forest camp (one which had clearly not extended to the club's supporters), the Reds were without Bob McKinlay and Colin Addison, both of whom were injured. Their places were taken by Billy Taylor and Bob Chapman.

Hull too brought in a last-minute replacement – forward Terry Heath, an £8,000 buy from Leicester City – and it was he who was to upstage his more illustrious team-mates.

The 10,000 Forest fans inside the splendid setting of Boothferry Park witnessed a jaded display from their heroes. Only Peter Grummitt in goal, the ageing Jeff Whitefoot and John Barnwell appeared to have the stomach for a fight. Alan Hinton made little headway on the left flank whereas his opposite number, the tall, elegant Butler, used the space to great effect. Forest never came to terms with Hull's formation in which, to accommodate Heath, leading scorer Houghton moved back to wing-half.

Houghton was pulling all the strings in midfield but Hull's first goal, after 20 minutes, owed more to a woeful defensive error than any creative play. Peter Hindley's back pass was too weak to reach Grummitt, allowing Heath to nip in and roll the ball under the prostrate keeper.

Wagstaff and Chilton were having an off day, both passing up presentable chances, so that the visitors remained very much in the game. They still struggled to manufacture any worthwhile openings although they did have loud penalty appeals rejected after Barry McArthur had been brought down. With time running out, Forest were dealt another blow when the unfortunate Hindley limped off, leaving them to soldier on with ten men. Then seven minutes from time, Heath made the game safe with his second strike. Chilton headed down Ray Henderson's cross from the right and Heath slipped a tackle before firing past Grummitt. It was no more than City deserved.

Hull City: Swan; Davidson, Brown, Jarvis, Milner, Houghton, Henderson, Wagstaff, Chilton, Heath, Butler.
Nottingham Forest: Grummitt; Hindley, Newton, Hennessey, Taylor, Whitefoot, Crowe, Chapman, McArthur, Barnwell, Hinton.
Referee: Mr J. Mitchell (Prescot)
Attendance: 38,000

53

Nuneaton Borough 2
Swansea Town 0

7 January 1967

'When Coughlin headed the ball back to Heyes, I ran in to challenge. I was about a yard away when Heyes picked up the ball. Then he glanced up at me and dropped it over the line.'

Nuneaton forward Tony Richards

*I*n charge at Manor Park for less than a year, manager Dudley Kernick had revitalised Southern Leaguers Nuneaton Borough. When he arrived, they were struggling against relegation but, having staved off that threat and following a summer overhaul of the playing staff, he had guided them to third place in the table. The directors responded by awarding him a five-year contract leading up to the second-round Cup tie with Third Division Swansea Town. For once, it was a vote of confidence which was not misplaced.

Swansea's international forward line, moulded around the crafts of Ivor Allchurch (winner of 68 Welsh caps), was an obvious threat. Despite eventually being relegated, they averaged almost two goals a game. As can be gathered, their defence was less impressive.

In front of a full house, Swansea's defence shook so much it could almost have been measured on the Richter scale. Borough's Paul Cutler had a second-minute scrambled effort disallowed and then when George Heyes dropped the ball under pressure from the same player, Vic Gomersall had to make a hasty clearance. With Swansea's defence in total disarray, Norman Ashe fired too high.

Swansea were a different matter altogether going forward. After Brian Evans had missed the target from 18 yards, he then headed a

125

McLaughlin cross over the top from a good position. It was a costly lapse. For Nuneaton went straight up to the other end and took a 22nd minute lead. Malcolm Allen slipped the ball out to Cutler whose cross was met by a beautiful glancing header from Tommy Crawley, leaving Heyes powerless to intercept. The goal repaid Dudley Kernick's faith. Crawley had been going through a lean spell in recent weeks and his place had been in jeopardy but Kernick persevered with him. Six minutes later, Swansea could have gone two down but Cutler, fed by Allen, dragged his shot wide with only Heyes to beat. They had a further escape four minutes from the break when Tony Richards' 20-yarder came back off the post with Heyes nothing more than a spectator.

In the second half, Crawley blazed wildly over following a fine solo run by Richards but then, after 65 minutes, came the comical goal which settled the issue. Swansea's Denis Coughlin tried to relieve the pressure by heading back to Heyes but the keeper dropped the ball and allowed it to trickle through his legs and over the line. It wasn't Coughlin's day. On 78 minutes, he thought he had pulled one back but his effort was disallowed for hands.

Swansea finished well beaten, allowing Nuneaton to progress to the third round where they lost to Rotherham after a replay. The Welshmen have continued to struggle against non-League opposition, going out to Margate, Kettering, Minehead, Bognor Regis Town and, in 1994, Nuneaton Borough again. It's a sad admission to have Nuneaton Borough as your bogey team.

Nuneaton Borough: Crump; Jones, Wilson, Davis, Watts, Allen, Ashe, Cutler, Richards, Crawley, Hails.
Swansea Town: Heyes; R. Evans, Gomersall, Coughlin, Purcell, Williams, Humphries, Todd, McLaughlin, Allchurch, B. Evans.
Referee: Mr R. Tinkler (Boston)
Attendance: 15,000

54

31 January 1967

*W*est Ham were the strawberry creams of football – pretty to look at but with a soft centre. They were always happier playing another First Division team rather than a side from the lower strata. Never was this more apparent than when, complete with their World Cup-winning heroes of the previous June – Bobby Moore, Geoff Hurst and Martin Peters – the Hammers took on Swindon Town in a third-round tie in 1967.

The first game at Upton Park ended in a thrilling 3-3 draw, Hurst bagging a hat-trick, and the replay took place at a packed County Ground three days later. For the replay, West Ham manager Ron Greenwood recalled former England forward Johnny Byrne and, more importantly, Ronnie Boyce returned for his first game since Boxing Day, having been laid low by an attack of shingles. Boyce was West Ham's engine room. With him in their side, they had scored 78 goals prior to Boxing Day; without him, they had managed just 11 in seven games. The Londoners saw Swindon as a good omen. They had beaten them in 1964 en route to winning the Cup.

But Swindon, under Danny Williams, were no country bumpkins. They were handily-placed in the Third Division and had a match-winner of their own in Don Rogers, a player whose popularity in Wiltshire surpassed even that of Dave Dee, Dozy, Beaky, Mick and Tich. Expectation was high that Tuesday night and some 2,000 spectators were locked out. Those who got in were not disappointed.

It was a cracking Cup tie. Swindon launched fast, furious attacks right from the start. After 18 minutes, Willie Penman collected the ball just inside the West Ham half and set off on a run for goal. Bobby

The Swindon players receive a heroes' welcome from jubilant fans.

Moore was screaming at his men to drop back and cover but before they could do so, Penman let fly with his right foot. The shot was charged down but dropped perfectly for Penman to hit with his left without breaking stride. This time it flew past the flat-footed Jim Standen into the net.

West Ham hit back strongly but Peters, Brian Dear and Byrne all squandered good chances. And they remained vulnerable to Swindon's lightning breaks, in one of which Roger Smart fed Rogers who shot just wide with Standen beaten. In the second half, Peters and Byrne frittered away further openings until Swindon finally succumbed to the pressure with 12 minutes to go. Dear's corner was headed away by Mel Nurse but only to John Sissons lurking on the edge of the box. Sissons' first-time shot gave the keeper no chance.

Many a team would have been deflated by this setback but Swindon roared straight back onto the attack. Six minutes later, full-back John Trollope brought the crowd to its feet with a storming run down the left and his chip to the far post dropped perfectly for the onrushing Rogers to take the ball on his thigh and sweep it high into the net. The *Evening Advertiser* noted the immediate effect of the goal. 'West Ham

128

suddenly looked a beaten team and even Moore appeared a tired and ordinary player.' There was no way back for the Hammers and a minute from the end, Penman retrieved a cross to the by-line and crossed for Ken Skeen to complete Swindon's night of glory. The occasion was not marred by any crowd trouble although the *Advertiser* remarked: 'There were a couple of incidents of indiscriminate parking in the Queen's Drive area, but these were isolated.' Hardly a matter for the FA...

Two years later, Swindon were to win the Football League Cup, another giant-killing feat disposing of Arsenal. West Ham continued to delight and frustrate in equal parts. In 1969, they crashed out of the FA Cup at Mansfield. They remained the team the minnows loved to play.

Swindon Town: Hicks; Thomas, Trollope, Morgan, Nurse, Harland, Brown, Smart, Skeen, Penman, Rogers.
West Ham United: Standen; Bovington, Burkett, Peters, Bickles, Moore, Dear, Boyce, Byrne, Hurst, Sissons.
Referee: Mr J.R. Osborne (Ipswich)
Attendance: 25,789

55

Tamworth 2
Torquay United 1

15 November 1969

'I wasn't at all worried about the result after I'd missed the penalty. I didn't think Torquay would equalise because we were playing so well. When I moved up to take the kick, I heard someone tell the keeper, "Go to your right" and he did.'

Tamworth's Dennis Smith

*D*ennis Smith was one of a breed of footballers which used to be popular with managers but extremely unpopular with supporters. They were called utility players. From the manager's point of view, they were invaluable because they could play in a number of different positions. To the supporter, they were a jack of all trades but master of none. So perhaps it should come as no surprise that Smith, barracked throughout the season by a section of Tamworth supporters, should miss a vital Cup tie penalty and promptly be named man-of-the-match by his manager, Hughie Morrow. Mind you, Morrow could afford to be in forgiving mood after seeing his humble West Midlands Regional League team out-think, outfight and outplay Third Division Torquay.

Despite their lowly status, Tamworth boasted plenty of League experience, particularly in defence. Back in 1962, Chuck Drury had played in a quarter-final for West Brom against Spurs and had been detailed to mark Jimmy Greaves. Greaves scored twice and Albion lost 4-2. Drury now drove a lorry. Tamworth's line-up also included a gas fitter (who probably charged double time for playing at weekends), an engineer, the usual painter and decorator and a couple of progress tracers. Their danger men were clay worker Graham Jessop and Ray Holmes who worked in a car factory. Between them, they had scored 43 goals that season (not bad going for mid-November) and Jessop alone had notched 67 in his last 85 matches. In the circumstances, Torquay manager Allan Brown wisely decided to watch Tamworth beforehand. Less wisely, he delayed it until a Midland Floodlit Cup tie a few days before the FA Cup. When the midweek game was called off, Brown and his team were left not knowing what to expect on the Saturday.

They soon discovered that Tamworth's secret weapon was the big boot of goalkeeper Johnny Crosby, used to propel the ball almost the length of the Kettlebrook pitch, thereby causing pandemonium in the Torquay ranks. Yet when John Rudge put Torquay ahead in the 20th minute, it seemed that League class would tell.

The turning point came after 62 minutes. Holmes and lightweight Torquay keeper Andy Donnelly went for a free-kick together.

Donnelly ended up on the floor, Holmes tapped the ball into the empty net, the referee gave a goal. Torquay protested bitterly but Holmes insisted later: 'It was a 50-50 ball. The keeper was slow coming for it and I got to it before him. It was a fair goal.'

Four minutes later, Tamworth were ahead. Roger Hope's right-wing corner sailed over the heads of the tall Torquay defenders for Jessop to nod in at the far post. The terrible twins had struck.

After Donnelly had saved Smith's 74th minute penalty, Torquay gained renewed heart. But it was not enough. After the match, Allan Brown hit out at two of his star players, Tommy Mitchinson, a £5,000 buy from Aston Villa, and Irish winger Eric Welsh, a £6,000 signing from Carlisle, over what he considered to be their poor work rate. And he was still none too happy about Tamworth's first goal.

Tamworth crashed 6-0 at Gillingham in the next round.

Tamworth: Crosby; Bache, Newton, Smith, Eden, Drury, Hope, Hall, Holmes, Jessop, Morrow.
Torquay United: Donnelly; Smyth, Kitchener, Glozier, Young, Dunne, Welsh, Cave, Rudge, Mitchinson, Scott.
Referee: Mr G. Trevett (Manchester)
Attendance: 4,080

56

Watford 1
Liverpool 0

21 February 1970

'I wouldn't say the best team won. I thought their goal came at the right moment for them. I thought Watford had shot their bolt but the goal lifted them. They hadn't the energy. It was more bravado

**which kept them going. In fact, I would go so far as to say Watford
are the worst team that's ever beaten us.'**

Liverpool boss Bill Shankly

*B**ill Shankly must have been rubbing his hands with delight when
the draw for the quarter-finals of the Cup was made. For
Liverpool had managed to avoid Manchester United, Chelsea and
Leeds and had been despatched instead to Vicarage Road, home of a
Watford side situated fourth from the foot of Division Two and
barely averaging a goal a game. The Kop regulars were already
dreaming of the semis.*

And who could blame them? Promoted as Third Division champions
the previous season, Watford had struggled to come to terms with the
higher grade. They were reasonably solid at the back (with Welsh
international Mike Walker, more recently manager at Norwich and
Everton, between the posts) but distinctly lacking in firepower, a
problem not remedied by the inclusion in the forward line of Mick
Packer, a player who, even in his faster paces, was only pedestrian.
Tricky winger Stewart Scullion was usually their best hope of a goal.
Nor did the Hertfordshire club boast any giant-killing tradition. More
often than not, they were on the receiving end against the likes of
Leytonstone, Walthamstow Avenue, Nuneaton Borough and Bedford
Town. Yet they had threatened to pull off the big one in recent
seasons. In 1967, they held Liverpool to a goalless draw at Vicarage
Road before losing the replay 3-1. In 1969, a Scullion goal earned
them a marvellous 1-1 draw at Old Trafford. Again they lost the
replay. And on their way to the last eight in 1970, they had already
accounted for First Division Stoke 1-0.

Even so, the Liverpool players must have thought they were on to a
good thing as they entered Vicarage Road with its quaint
connotations of croquet and crumpets. A menacing Anfield-like sign
declaring 'THIS IS VICARAGE ROAD' would have been somewhat
wasted.

Complacency was to prove Liverpool's downfall. There can be no
other explanation for an absymal performance which, as *The Times*

remarked, permitted Watford an easier game than most of their Second Division encounters. Without Tommy Smith and Peter Thompson, Liverpool looked a pale imitation. The well-oiled machine was clogged up. Ron Yeats, a perennial colossus at the back, was a nervous wreck, dragged all over the place by Barry Endean, a player picked up from Durham Sunday League football. Only Ian St John played up to his reputation, apart from the occasional flash from Bobby Graham on the wing. The no-nonsense Watford defenders restricted Liverpool to speculative long-range efforts, borne out by the fact that the visitors' best attempt was a fierce 35-yard drive from the otherwise ineffective Alun Evans, turned over the bar by Walker.

By contrast, Watford, quicker in the tackle and more penetrative up front, had the man-of-the-match in midfield player Ray Lugg, not the sort of name to adorn too many bedroom walls. After 15 minutes, by which time Terry Garbett had already driven into the side netting, Lugg produced a pinpoint cross which was headed wastefully over the top by the onrushing Brian Owen. Scullion and Endean were both narrowly off target as half-time approached before Lugg's service finally reaped greater reward in the 62nd minute. Just after clearing his own lines following Walker's half-save from Graham, Lugg was at the other end to nutmeg Peter Wall out on the right. He then sent over an enticing cross and Endean found space at the near post to plant a solid header through the flailing fingers of Tommy Lawrence.

To Watford's credit, they refused to sit back on their lead or indulge in any time-wasting. Emlyn Hughes had a fleeting chance to equalise but, as with most of his TV appearances, he was sadly off target. And after an agonising four minutes of injury time, Watford were in the semi-finals for the first time in their history.

Back in December when the third-round draw had sent his side to Bolton, Watford boss Ken Furphy had said, tongue-in-cheek perhaps: 'Bolton away – well, these are the sort of teams you have to beat if you want to get to Wembley.' Everybody laughed. Nobody was laughing now. Least of all Liverpool.

57

Colchester United 3
Leeds United 2

13 February 1971

*L*eeds United under Don Revie. Intensely professional. Respected *rather than loved. The most consistent team in the land. League Champions in 1969, runners-up in the League and Cup in 1970, League runners-up in 1971 and 1972, Cup winners in 1972 and finalists in 1973. So what happened to the Cup in 1971? As Clive Tyldesley would say: 'Colchester United – that's what happened.'*

Little Colchester. A combination of ageing pros and journeymen footballers (among them left-back Bobby Cram, uncle of Steve), leading a leisurely existence in the middle of the Fourth Division. Six of their team were over 30. But the club had a Cup pedigree stretching back to 1948 and, remarkably, had never lost to a First Division team at Layer Road. Huddersfield, Arsenal and West Bromwich Albion had all failed to win on Essex soil. However Leeds were a different proposition. Three points clear at the top of the First Division, even without the injured Billy Bremner, they would surely have no trouble in removing Colchester from their path to Wembley. They were like robots, programmed to win or, if not, draw. They did not appear to possess the human frailties required to become the victims of a giant-killing.

Colchester's Cup campaign had begun against slightly more modest

Colchester match-winners Ray Crawford (left) and Dave Simmons kiss the boots which destroyed Leeds.

opposition, Sussex County Leaguers Ringmer. They had subsequently knocked out Cambridge United, Barnet and Rochdale (after a replay), bringing their goals total to 15. So they knew they could score goals and boasted an experienced marksman in 34-year-old Ray Crawford, the former Ipswich and England man. Crawford reckoned he had the Indian sign on Leeds. He had netted eight times against them in the past and, whilst not predicting that Colchester would win, he did go as far as to state that he would definitely score. The Colchester manager was Dick Graham, one of the old school, a man whose fierce crew-cut suggested he would have been more at home on the parade ground than the training ground. He devised a game plan whereby John Kurila and John Gilchrist were to do man-for-man marking jobs on Allan Clarke and Johnny Giles respectively. 'If Clarke and Giles went to the toilet,' said Graham afterwards, 'I wanted my two men there as well!'

In a rash moment, Graham had also promised to scale the walls of Colchester Castle if his team won. Even he must have doubted that his climbing skills would be put to the test. They came from all around. Those who could not get into the tiny ground perched in surrounding trees. From what happened in the next 55 minutes, it

135

was a wonder they did not come crashing down from the branches in stunned amazement.

Leeds were simply unrecognisable from the machine we had come to expect. In *The Times*, a disbelieving Geoffrey Green described how Crawford and Dave Simmons reduced Jackie Charlton to 'a dithering novice'; how the inspirational Brian Lewis switched wings to confuse Paul Reaney and Terry Cooper; and how Gilchrist 'reduced Giles to a mere name in the programme'. Only Norman Hunter of the much-vaunted Leeds defence was on his game.

United's chief destroyer was their old bogey man, Ray Crawford. After 18 minutes, Lewis floated over a free-kick from the left, Gary Sprake flapped at it and missed, leaving Crawford a free header at the far post. To be ahead against Leeds was excitement enough for the Colchester fans but they could scarcely believe their eyes when Crawford scored again ten minutes later. Crawford beat Reaney in the air and, as he fell to the ground, hooked home the loose ball via a post with Sprake stranded, the whole sequence of events seeming to take place in slow motion.

Colchester looked dangerous whenever they attacked but must have expected that a tongue-lashing from Revie would see a revitalised Leeds after the break. So when it became 3-0 in 55 minutes, the fans must have thought they were dreaming. A long lob down the middle by Lewis caught Sprake and Reaney in four minds, allowing Simmons to nip between them and head into the empty net.

In a desperate last throw of the dice, Revie moved Clarke back into midfield and pushed Giles into attack. This threatened to disrupt Graham's plan since his instructions to Kurila and Gilchrist to swap accordingly couldn't be heard above the crowd. With Colchester in a state of confusion, Hunter headed home Peter Lorimer's corner in the 60th minute. Fifteen minutes later, it was panic stations when Giles converted a flick from Mick Jones to make it 3-2. It seemed that Colchester might cave in completely but somehow they held on. Then Lorimer drove a low cross into the goalmouth. Jones connected from almost point-blank range, only for keeper Graham Smith to pull off a superb reflex save. He may have made better saves in his career but none as important. For in that moment, Colchester were through to the sixth round and Dick Graham was hunting out his crampons.

'Miracles are rare and must be savoured: this one in particular will have its place in memory. Great-grandchildren will hear tell of it.'

Geoffrey Green in The Times

58

Hereford United 2
Newcastle United 1

5 February 1972

*F*or the first time since Yeovil's victory over Sunderland in 1949, a First Division team was knocked out of the Cup by a non-League club. Hereford's triumph, epitomised by Ronnie Radford's amazing goal, has become such a part of FA Cup folklore that it has tended to obscure two facts about this third-round tie – that Hereford's winning goal was actually scored by Ricky George and that it came in a replay.

It was on 24 January that Hereford, second in the Southern League, earned a highly creditable 2-2 draw at St James's Park, a match they considered themselves unlucky not to have won. The two teams spent the next 12 days kicking their heels as heavy rain turned Hereford's Edgar Street Pitch into a quagmire. 'Our pitch wasn't the

The Hereford players are mobbed by supporters following the epic triumph over First Division Newcastle.

best,' said Hereford player/manager Colin Addison afterwards. 'It only needed a shower and you couldn't play.' It was Newcastle who suffered most. Joe Harvey and his team spent ten days cooped up in a Hereford hotel as postponement followed postponement. Away from their families, the Newcastle players were further inconvenienced by the lack of training facilities in the area. They tried the concrete surface of a nearby RAF station and even muddy Worcester racecourse. It was scarcely the ideal preparation for such a tricky game.

The match finally got the go-ahead on fourth-round day. Hereford were ready and waiting. They needed no motivation – Newcastle's Malcolm Macdonald, never noted for his reticence, saw to that. Colin Addison explained: 'After we had drawn up there, Macdonald said in the papers that Hereford had had their moment of glory and that he would score ten in the replay. I simply pinned that article on our dressing-room wall.'

In spite of the delay, Newcastle made the better start. Twice in the opening half, they hit the bar and forced the first six corners of the game. But with the slope in their favour, Hereford fought back with a vengeance in the second half. Former Arsenal player Addison was controlling midfield while McLaughlin kept Macdonald in check. But then after 82 minutes, very much against the run of play, Viv Busby crossed from the right and Macdonald rose to head home.

That seemed to be it, but *The Times* correspondent noted one Hereford player shaking his fists and clapping his hands to gee-up his teammates as they trooped back to the centre circle. That man was Ronnie Radford. Four minutes later, Radford played a one-two with Brian Owen and unleashed a 40-yard rocket which roared into Iam McFaul's top right-hand corner. McFaul was not the tallest goalkeeper in the world but even Twizzle wouldn't have got near that shot. In 67 games for Newport, Radford had scored just seven times. He had joined Hereford the previous summer. It was only his third goal of the season.

Hereford dominated extra-time. Full-back Roger Griffiths, who, it later transpired, had played nearly 80 minutes with a fracture of the left fibula, limped off and was replaced by Ricky George. On 102 minutes, George became the FA Cup's most celebrated substitute when, accepting a short pass from Radford, he slithered a shot across McFaul and inside the far post.

Eighteen minutes later, the celebrations began in earnest and carried on for four days. They were suspended for the fourth-round clash with West Ham on the Wednesday. The game at Edgar Street ended in a goalless draw with West Ham going on to win the replay 3-1. Hereford may have lost the battle but they had won the war, having done enough to gain admission to the Football League the following season. Who could resist their entry after the way in which they had captured the nation's hearts one grey afternoon in February?

Hereford United: Potter; Griffiths (George), Mallender, Jones, McLaughlin, Addison, Gough, Tyler, Meadows, Owen, Radford.
Newcastle United: McFaul; Craig, Clark, Nattrass, Howard, Moncur, Busby, Green, Macdonald, Tudor, Hibbitt.
Referee: Mr D. Turner (Cannock)
Attendance: 15,000

'When we weathered the first 20 minutes, we knew we stood a chance. Dudley Tyler started to run them ragged and they became wary. We were kicking down the slope in the second half – we preferred it that way – and even when they scored, we wouldn't lie down. We had such a terrific team spirit. I won the ball in midfield with John Tudor and played a one-two with Brian Owen. The return pass came off Brian's shin. It sat there, just waiting to be hit. Colin Addison shouted, "My ball, Raddy" but then he slipped so I went for it. I just hit it and it flew in. I'd done it before and since but the difference was, that was on TV. Once we'd equalised, Newcastle had gone. After all, a few minutes earlier, they thought they'd won it.'

Hereford goal-scoring hero Ronnie Radford

59

Sunderland 1
Leeds United 0

5 May 1973

*I*t was the biggest Cup Final upset since Blackburn, struggling against relegation, had beaten double-chasing Huddersfield in 1928. Yet a few months earlier, the likelihood of Sunderland winning any trophy in the foreseeable future – even Quiz Ball – appeared distinctly remote. The north-east's fading giants had been faced with the grim prospect of relegation to Division Three for the first time in their history. Then Bob Stokoe was appointed manager. He turned their whole season around. They began to climb the table, eventually finishing sixth, and embarked on a run which was to see off Notts County, Reading, Manchester City, Luton and Arsenal on the road to Wembley.

Don Revie's Leeds were back to their best after the Colchester debacle. They were the Cup holders and red-hot favourites to retain the trophy. History was with them too. No Second Division team had won the Cup for 42 years. But Stokoe had become something of a Messiah on Wearside. The Sunderland fans believed he could achieve anything. Most neutrals certainly hoped he could put a spanner in the Leeds works.

It was an emotional rather than a great final. The best run of the entire afternoon was made by Stokoe at the final whistle. Prior to that, there were only two memorable incidents – the goal and the double save.

The goal arrived on the half-hour. A corner from Billy Hughes on the left was met by centre-half Dave Watson. As the ball dropped, Ian Porterfield killed the bounce with his left thigh and lashed the ball into the net with his rarely-used right foot. The save came in the 70th minute. Leeds, who had a 55th-minute penalty appeal turned down, were enjoying their most productive period of the match. Paul Reaney got the ball out on the right and crossed deep into the goalmouth where Trevor Cherry stooped to plant a firm header towards the far corner. Jim Montgomery reacted swiftly to palm it out but the ball only travelled as far as Peter Lorimer, possessor of the hardest shot in football. From no more than six yards, Lorimer let rip. Montgomery was still on the ground but, in that split second as the ball hurtled towards him, he instinctively put up an arm and managed to divert the shot onto the bar and away to safety. The Leeds players held their heads in disbelief. With that save, their hopes died.

It was no more than Sunderland deserved. Micky Horswill had shadowed Giles from start to finish and little skipper Bobby Kerr had run himself into the ground, helping to subdue Leeds' danger man, Eddie Gray. It was so effective that Gray was eventually substituted by Terry Yorath. Giles and Billy Bremner were sadly lacking in ideas, resorting to lofting high balls into the Sunderland area where they were eagerly gobbled up by the towering figure of centre-half Dave Watson. In fact, Sunderland nearly added a second in the last minute, David Harvey making a sprawling save from Vic Halom after Kerr and the lively Dennis Tueart had sliced through the Leeds defence.

(right) *Sunderland boss Bob Stokoe in a change of headgear as he holds the Cup aloft.*
(below) *The goal that did it. Ian Porterfield (stripes, right) turns away after burying the ball past Leeds' David Harvey.*

As referee Ken Burns blew the final whistle, Bob Stokoe, resplendent in his trilby, raced across the pitch to hug his hero, Jim Montgomery. He may have lacked the grace and speed of Linford Christie but for Stokoe, it was a personal best. Besides, Christie has never had to run the 100 metres in a hat and coat.

There was no doubt who was the Sunderland fans' hero: Stokoe. And they refused to leave the stadium until he came over to see them. Perhaps his mind flashed back to the 1955 final when he was centre-half in the Newcastle team which beat Manchester City. The City centre-forward he blotted out that day was Don Revie.

'Towards the end, my nerves were shot to bits. The ball was pinging around our area and I was convinced we had another four or five minutes to hold on. As Ken Burns ran by, I asked him how long there was to go. He just gave me a big grin and said: "It's alright, Bobby, you've won it." Twenty seconds later he blew the whistle, and we had.'

Sunderland captain Bobby Kerr

60

Exeter City 0
Alvechurch 1

24 November 1973

'I still can't believe it. Our plan was to attack whenever we could and then defend like dervishes. And that is what we did.'

Alvechurch manager Wyn Bowen

*E*xeter City were going through a bad patch in 1973. It had lasted best part of 40 years. So the Fourth Division side were mightily relieved when the first-round Cup draw delivered them nothing more exacting than a visit from some team called Alvechurch.

Nobody even knew where Alvechurch was. It transpired that they were Worcestershire village amateurs who played in the Premier Division of the Midland Combination alongside clubs with lots of initials like G.K.N. Sankey, not to mention Hereford United Reserves,

Brereton Social and Brierley Hill Athletic. They had made a brief appearance in the first round proper two years earlier, losing 4-2 at Aldershot. It was not exactly a pedigree to strike fear into the opposition.

The first half offered little hint of an upset. Alvechurch keeper Ward was called into action to make good saves from Wallace and West Country folk hero Fred Binney but had a lucky escape in the 26th minute when Wallace missed a sitter, hooking wide of the goal from five yards out when completely unmarked.

Alvechurch's main threat was carried by Graham Allner and when he was brought down in the second half, the away fans were baying for a penalty. The referee would have none of it. With the minutes ticking away, Exeter threw caution to the wind in a bid to snatch the winner and so avoid a replay. As yet another attack broke down, Ward gathered the ball and threw it out to Deehan. With Exeter committed upfield, he produced a superb pass which took out a home defender and released Allner running through on the blind side. Keeping his composure, Allner rolled the ball gently past the advancing Wilson, the ball seeming to take an eternity to cross the line.

And so Alvechurch brought off a wonderful victory. The *Sunday Mercury* enthused: 'Several fans and players had tears in their eyes at the final whistle. The players were mobbed in a sea of black and amber. The 500 fans looked and sounded like 5,000.'

Alvechurch went on to crush King's Lynn 6-1 in the second round before bowing out 4-2 at Bradford City. But the FA Cup had not heard the last of Graham Allner. In 1994, he was to steer Kidderminster Harriers to an equally famous triumph at Birmingham City.

Exeter City: Wilson; Crawford, Blain, Joy, Giles, Clapham, Wallace, Binney, Plumb, Neale, Wingate.
Alvechurch: Ward; Lyne, Tunsheon, Francis, Bayliss, Deehan, Clements, Palmer, Allner, Lawrance, Horne.
Attendance: 4,686

61

Brighton & Hove Albion 0
Walton & Hersham 4

28 November 1973

*I*t was the clash soccer had been waiting for. The team managed by
Brian Clough against the club from Julie Andrews's home town.
Brighton under Clough were a shambles – and he knew it. They had
finished bottom of the Second Division the previous season and spent
most of the 1973-74 campaign hovering dangerously above the Third
Division relegation zone. Among their more spectacular setbacks was
an 8-2 home defeat by Bristol Rovers. Isthmian Leaguers Walton had
won the Amateur Cup the previous year but had little FA Cup history
to speak of, never having progressed beyond the second round. They
had a well-drilled side, including a tigerish tackler in midfield by the
name of Dave Bassett. So Walton, whose only other League victims
were Exeter the year before, relished the opportunity of a home first-
round tie with Cloughie's men. It ended in a goalless draw. Walton,
labelled 'highly competent amateurs' by Clough, were unfortunate
not to win.

The replay at the Goldstone Ground saw Brighton dominate the first
20 minutes. It seemed that League class would tell. But then the
Seagulls were shocked from a great height by a Walton goal. From a
corner by Smith, Lambert flicked the ball on for Perkins to sink to his
knees and head past the floundering Powney. Brighton came back
strongly but, with Edwards standing firm at the heart of the Walton
defence, chances were at a premium. One fell to former Chelsea and
England striker Barry Bridges but he fell over and missed the ball
from less than a yard out. Just before the hour, Walton nearly made
the game safe. Clive Foskett rounded the keeper but lost control at the
vital moment, allowing Templeman to block his mis-hit shot.

As the minutes ticked away, Brighton poured forward – but with all the planning and co-ordination of lemmings rather than the fifth cavalry. With all the Brighton players bar Powney in the Walton half, it was only a matter of time before they were caught out. Sure enough, a Brighton shot was charged down and rebounded to Perkins who, along with Foskett, had anticipated the break and had started to run before the Brighton defenders were able to retreat. The pair found themselves ten yards inside their own half but with only Powney between them and the Brighton goal. Bearing down on the hapless Powney, Perkins held the ball until Foskett peeled away to the right. A simple pass, a cool finish and Walton were two up.

The game was now lost but still Brighton threw men upfield in a suicide mission. After 84 minutes, Woffinden's huge clearance sent Foskett on a clear run to goal. Powney came sprinting out and Foskett calmly rounded him and scored. A few minutes later, Morris led another break and laid on an easy chance for Foskett to round off a quick-fire hat-trick. Brighton's humiliation was complete.

To show that it was no fluke, the following season Brighton lost at home to Leatherhead whose team boasted super-confident Chris Kelly, the self-styled 'Leatherhead Lip'. By then, Cloughie had gone.

The usually shy and retiring Dave Bassett (front row, third from the right) leads the Walton & Hersham celebrations.

The sea air had not been to his liking. Julie's boys had seen to that.

> **Brighton & Hove Albion:** Powney; Templeman, Ley, Spearritt, Gall, Piper (Towner), Bridges, Howell, Hilton, Robertson, O'Sullivan.
> **Walton & Hersham:** Bloom; Sargent, Lambert, Donaldson, Edwards, Bassett, Woffinden, Smith, Perkins, Foskett, Morris.
> **Referee:** Mr G. Kew (Amersham)
> **Attendance:** 9,657

'Walton were better than us at every aspect of the game – better technique, certainly, and better organisation.'

Brian Clough

62

Burnley 0
Wimbledon 1

4 January 1975

*J**ust over a year after helping Walton & Hersham destroy Brighton, Dave Bassett popped up again in another giant-killing side. He was in good company. For joining him in the Wimbledon line-up were two other Walton heroes, Donaldson and Edwards, plus geography teacher Mickey Mahon who had starred in Colchester's defeat of Leeds. And rather like a shark and blood, once these chaps had got the taste of giant-killing, they were desperate for more.*

Home victories over fellow Southern Leaguers Bath and Kettering had earned Wimbledon a tough third-round tie at First Division Burnley, managed by Jimmy Adamson who had skippered the Lancashire club against Spurs in the 1962 Cup Final. Burnley were now lying seventh in the table and, with 45 goals, were the division's leading scorers. The source of most of their goals was Welsh international winger Leighton James who, on his day, was a handful for any defender in the country. Although a respectable third in the Southern League, Wimbledon knew that history was against them. The last non-League team to win away to a First Division side was Darlington back in 1920. And even Dave Bassett wasn't around then!

Burnley watched Wimbledon three times before the match. On two of those occasions, Wimbledon lost. Meanwhile the Dons' manager, Allen Batsford, was preparing his own version of *War and Peace* – a 15-page dossier on Burnley. On the morning of the game, Batsford and his coach Brian Hall put their ideas into practice on a Burnley sports ground. Yet for all the attention to detail, the ultimate success of the scheme relied heavily on an inspirational performance from one man – Wimbledon goalkeeper Dickie Guy.

Having failed to make the grade at League level, Guy worked as a tally clerk at London docks. He had not missed a match for Wimbledon for four years. He was called into action as early as the third minute, brilliantly plucking out of the air a cross-shot from Paul Fletcher. Leighton James was the subject of close attention from the Wimbledon players. Full-back Bob Stockley occasionally summoned reinforcements to deal with him, and Bassett was sternly lectured after hacking down the winger. Burnley continued to look menacing. On 27 minutes, Guy superbly saved Ray Hankin's header from James's cross and, three minutes later, he grabbed a powerful volley from Keith Newton at the second attempt. Wimbledon's only threat in the first period was a high cross-cum-shot from Billy Edwards which Alan Stevenson turned over the bar.

Four minutes into the second half, much of Turf Moor fell silent. It was a reverence usually only reserved for Bob Lord. Bank clerk Ian Cooke forced his way past Burnley full-back Jim Thomson and managed to get in a shot. It was charged down by Stevenson but the ball ran loose along the edge of the box. Roger Connell took a swing at it and miscued but following up was Mickey Mahon who made no mistake with a sweetly-struck left-foot drive. Mahon said afterwards: 'I thought Roger Connell would get in the way and there wasn't a lot of goal to aim at but it went straight in. I will never forget the look on the faces of the Burnley team when we scored.'

Keiron Somers had two chances to increase Wimbledon's lead on the break but, predictably enough, most of the drama was at the other end as Burnley strove for an equaliser. Guy pulled off a number of fine stops, saving his most heart-stopping moment for the final minute when he spilled Fletcher's shot. Fortunately for Wimbledon, Doug Collins fired the rebound over the top.

The Dons nearly claimed an even bigger scalp in the next round. Following a 0-0 draw at Elland Road, in which Guy saved a Lorimer penalty, they lost the replay 1-0, Leeds' winning goal being deflected in off Bassett, the man destined to become Wimbledon's manager.

Back to Burnley and the only blot on Wimbledon's day was when the jubilant players returned to the coach to find that it had been broken into during the course of the game. But, in what was to typify the Wimbledon spirit in years to come, they simply laughed it off. Who needs a Moira Anderson cassette anyway?

Burnley: Stevenson; Newton, Thomson (Morris), Ingham, Waldron, Noble, Flynn, Hankin, Fletcher, Collins, James.
Wimbledon: Guy; Stockley, Bryant, Donaldson, Edwards, Bassett, Cooke, Rice, Connell, Somers, Mahon.
Referee: Mr R.B. Lee (Cheadle)
Attendance: 19,683

'I don't think they realised we could play so well. Club coach Brian Hall and I were up till two o'clock this morning scrapping, then reconsidering ideas as to how we could beat them. It might have been different if Bob Stockley had been skinned three times by Leighton James in the first ten minutes, but he wasn't. We worked out that they got their attacks to a certain point, usually on either flank, and then used the cross. We had to stop them reaching this stage or deal with the crosses. It went as planned. They were too predictable.'

Wimbledon manager Allen Batsford delivering his after-match verdict

63

22 November 1975

'I hate poached eggs but that's what we've had before the last two Cup rounds, so it had to be the same again.'

Coventry Sporting full-back Charlie Sorbie, bowing to tradition

*T*hey're a superstitious bunch, footballers. They won't drink 13 pints of lager on the morning of a match nor walk under a black cat on the way to the ground. Coventry Sporting were no exception. For their first-round tie with Tranmere, Manager David Kite insisted on wearing his lucky tie with its Bill Glazier Testimonial Fund emblem (Glazier was a Coventry City goalkeeper of the 1960s); midfield player Tony Dunk wore his lucky gold crucifix (at least he left the medallion at home); all the players sat in the same places for the hotel meal as they had in the qualifying rounds; and Charlie Sorbie tucked into his poached eggs.

One could understand Sporting not wishing to take any chances. It was, after all, the biggest day in the little West Midlands Regional League club's 30-year history, the first time they had ever reached the first round proper of the FA Cup. And they had hired Coventry City's Highfield Road ground specially for the occasion.

Tranmere were riding high in the Fourth Division, having been relegated the previous season. Away ties with non-Leaguers appeared to hold little fear for them. In recent years, they had travelled to, and vanquished, Skelmersdale United, South Liverpool and Farsley Celtic. One of Rovers' scorers against Farsley Celtic in 1974 had been a promising young winger by the name of Steve Coppell. But he had since moved on to Old Trafford.

David Kite was by no means in awe of Tranmere's record and spent the week prior to the match telling anyone who would listen that Sporting would win 2-0. Russell Grant would have been proud of him.

There were 11 heroes in the part-timers' line-up that afternoon but two are worthy of special mention. Goalkeeper Howard Jeavons, a 29-year-old fitter, had been with the club for 14 years. Two years earlier, he had suffered a double fracture of the leg and was out of the game for 14 months amidst fears that he might never play again. Against Tranmere, he was superb, although he was greatly assisted by a sound back four of Sorbie, Derek Jones, Simon Skelcey and Bob Mundy who combined to ensure that Tranmere's prolific marksman, Ronnie Moore, saw only the occasional glimpses of goal.

While Jeavons kept a clean sheet at one end, two-goal Stuart Gallagher was making a name for himself at the other. On 40 minutes, Dunk took a free-kick out on the left and when the ball came over, Gallagher nipped in to prod it into the net off a post. He doubled his team's tally in the 80th minute, moments after seeing a fine header hit the bar. This time, Jackie Manning swung over a high cross and the lean figure of Gallagher got up between defender Dave Philpotts and keeper Dick Johnson to head into the unguarded net. Basking in the glory, Gallagher said afterwards: 'I dreamt on Friday night that I had played well and we had won. Now I can hardly believe that we've actually done it. What a weekend it's been for me. I came out of my apprenticeship, it was my 20th birthday and we're through to the second round.'

The second-round draw brought a visit from Peterborough United. Sporting were naturally optimistic. They lost 4-0. Maybe the eggs were off.

Coventry Sporting: Jeavons; Sorbie, Jones, Skelcey, Mundy, Dunk, Starkey, Manning, Gore, Gallagher, Randle.
Tranmere Rovers: Johnson; Matthias, Griffiths, Philpotts, Parry, Tynan, Mitchell, Young, Kenny, Peplow, Moore.
Attendance: 4,565

64

Norwich City 1
Bradford City 2

23 February 1976

*J*ohn Bond could be his own biggest enemy. There were times when *he was to diplomacy what Michael Foot was to high fashion. So when the Norwich boss dismissed Bradford City as 'muddlers' before their fifth-round tie, he couldn't have given the Fourth Division outfit a greater incentive to win. Not for the first time, nor the last, Bond's words backfired on him.*

Bradford certainly needed some form of stimulus. They were down amongst the League's dead men (they eventually finished 17th in Division Four) and were expected to be no match for a Norwich side which, although struggling against relegation from the First Division, possessed some quality performers. The bad feeling between the clubs was heightened when Bradford, who had seven first-teamers out with 'flu, twice successfully applied to have the tie postponed. Bond was annoyed. He wanted the Cup match resolved one way or the other so that he could attend to Norwich's League position.

When the game finally got under way, Norwich seemed in a hurry to get it over with. Crosses aimed at Ted MacDougall and Martin Peters forced Bradford to defend desperately with keeper Peter Downsborough being called upon to make a number of fine saves, most notably in the 30th minute to halt a header from full-back David Jones. It wasn't Jones's day. Eight minutes later, it was his mistake which enabled Bradford to take a shock lead – one, which on the balance of play, they scarcely merited. Jones sent a pass straight into the path of Bradford's Don Hutchins and immediately tried to redeem himself by bringing the winger down. However Hutchins hurdled the challenge and unleashed a strong, swerving, dipping shot from the edge of the area. Utterly bamboozled by the wayward flight, Norwich keeper Kevin Keelan could only help the ball into the net. It was only the third time he had touched the ball in the entire match.

Within two minutes, Norwich were level, Peters neatly back-heading in a left-wing corner from Colin Suggett. Norwich swarmed forward in the minutes before the interval and Downsborough had to be at his most alert to deny Colin Sullivan and Phil Boyer.

The second half was much the same story. Cec Podd cleared off the line from Peters and, in the space of a minute, both Dave Stringer and Duncan Forbes struck the Bradford woodwork. Norwich threw everything at Downsborough except the kitchen sink and, on this form, he would probably have stopped that too – or at least have known a good plumber who could. Then with just three minutes remaining, Norwich shot themselves in the foot again. This time the culprit was the usually dependable Stringer, making his 500th appearance for the Canaries. His casual side-footed pass was seized upon by 21-year-old Billy McGinley, a free transfer signing from Huddersfield. McGinley ran into the box and aimed for goal. His shot was blocked by Sullivan but, not to be denied, the youngster picked up the rebound and fired home through Keelan's legs.

So Bradford became only the third Division Four side to reach the last eight of the FA Cup, the first time the club had done so for 56 years. Meanwhile Norwich, those famous giant-killers of the past, were left to reflect on what it was like to be on the receiving end. And John Bond was heard to be considering a vow of silence.

Norwich City: Keelan; Jones, Sullivan, McGuire, Forbes, Stringer, Machin, MacDougall, Boyer, Suggett, Peters.
Bradford City: Downsborough; Podd, Cooper, Johnson, Middleton, Fretwell, McGinley, Ingram, Cooke, D .Hall, Hutchins.
Referee: Mr J. Homewood (Sunbury-on-Thames)
Attendance: 27,047

'The defender went in awkwardly. I just got a lucky break. Gerry Ingram was in the goal area and I was in two minds whether to pass it to him, but I just got in the box and hit it. The ball hit a defender and the two of them left it to each other so I hit it back through the goalkeeper's legs.'

Billy McGinley

65

15 December 1976

'My problem is that where I drive my Coal Board lorry, everyone is a Mansfield supporter. I don't know what they'll say to me now.'

Brian Arblaster, goalkeeper for part-timers Matlock

*P*romoted as Fourth Division champions the previous season, Mansfield went into this tie boasting an unbeaten home record stretching back 12 months. However the Field Mill diehards were always wary about taking on non-League opposition, remembering only too well the 5-1 humiliation at Northern Leaguers Tow Law Town back in 1967.

For Matlock, it was their first-ever appearance on a Football League ground and their debut in the second round of the Cup. Events dictated that they would not forget it in a hurry. They too were enjoying a successful season – albeit in the Northern Premier League – and were unbeaten since September. Their game revolved around the three Fenoughty brothers – player/manager Tom, brother Mick and the youngest of the trio, Nick. It was the latter who was to prove Mansfield's destroyer-in-chief.

The tie had twice been postponed – first on account of a frozen pitch and then for fog – and it turned out to be a case of third time unlucky for Mansfield.

The opening minutes gave little hint of the drama to come but then on 21 minutes, the Derbyshire team took a shock lead. Full-back Dave Goodwin joined the attack and hit a shot which barely possessed sufficient power to dislodge a grazing ladybird. It certainly appeared to pose no threat to the Mansfield goal until a crazy deflection sent the ball spinning wide of the helpless Rod Arnold.

The misfortune was forgotten 11 minutes later when Matthews squeezed home an equaliser, only for Nick Fenoughty to restore the visitors' advantage within 60 seconds, rounding off a smart move.

Mansfield's hopes of pegging back the deficit in the second half were nearly dealt a killer blow less than a minute after the restart. Nick Fenoughty's shot hit a post and rebounded into the arms of the grateful Arnold. Mansfield then began to turn up the heat, only to be thwarted by former Sheffield United and Chesterfield keeper Brian Arblaster. In the space of two minutes, he pulled off three breathtaking saves – one from Miller and two from Kevin Randall. Finally on 62 minutes he was beaten by a Colin Foster header and Mansfield were back on level terms.

Fearing a Mansfield onslaught, Matlock showed the first signs of nerves and referee Terry Bosi had to warn them for time-wasting. As far as Mansfield were concerned, it turned out to be the worst thing he could have done for almost immediately, in the 64th minute, Nick Fenoughty was on the spot to finish off a move started by brother Mick and carried on by Peter Scott.

Mansfield had used up all their escape cards now and could only look on helplessly as Colin Oxley (83 minutes) and Scott (89 minutes) gave the scoreline a decisive, if somewhat flattering, look.

Matlock's dreams of landing a big club in the third round were shattered when the balls in the bag sent them to Carlisle. To make matters worse, they crashed 5-1. It would be another 12 years before they next appeared in the first round proper.

66

Stoke City 2
Blyth Spartans 3

6 February 1978

In 1923, Blyth Spartans were knocked out of the Cup at the first-round stage by Stoke City. In 1978, the two teams met again. The word around the north-east was that some of the Blyth players had been waiting a long time to get their revenge.

After beating Enfield in the third round, Blyth were in uncharted territory. Even though they were second in the Northern League, they faced difficult opponents in Stoke who held a place in the top half of the Second Division and paraded experienced professionals in Howard Kendall, Terry Conroy and Viv Busby, the latter knowing all about giant-killing after being in the Newcastle team which lost at Hereford. In Busby's case, lightning was to strike twice. Indeed, heavy rain caused the tie to be postponed for ten days although Blyth's Keith Houghton, a Wallsend policeman, did get in some match practice by playing for Northumbria Police against Strathclyde Police on the day before he took the field at Stoke.

Blyth's performance at Stoke was an economy of effort. Three serious attacks brought three goals. On 11 minutes, Stoke keeper Roger Jones stretched to catch Robert Carney's corner but the ball slithered out of his grasp straight to Terry Johnson who slid home from a couple of yards. After only 30 seconds, Busby had rounded Blyth keeper Clarke before recklessly shooting into the side netting and now Stoke set about their task with gusto. Conroy went agonisingly close and then Kendall's shot was half-saved by Clarke, the ball eventually being headed off the line by Ron Guthrie, a member of Sunderland's 1973 Cup winning team.

A Stoke equaliser had to come and did. In the 57th minute, a free-kick ricocheted to Busby who found the far corner of the net from 15 yards. Six minutes later, Stoke took the lead. Conroy's corner was headed on by Busby for Garth Crooks to nod in at the far post. The training ground had reaped its award and surely Blyth were on their way out now. Yet incredibly, with 15 minutes remaining, they too scored from a set-piece, although one which will never be found in any soccer manual. Guthrie's free-kick bounced off the Stoke wall and spun wildly towards goal. As the Stoke defenders stood dumbfounded, no fewer than five Blyth forwards pursued the ball. It hit the left-hand post and rebounded to Alan Shoulder who promptly headed it against the opposite post. This time it came back to Steve Carney who joyously fired home.

For Stoke, the worst was yet to come. In the very last minute, Blyth won a free-kick out on the right. John Waterson seemed to have over-hit it but Houghton managed to head back towards Robert Carney. He stuck out a foot, diverting the ball to the unmarked Johnson who hammered the ball into the net to the delight and disbelief of the band of travelling Blyth fans.

As the result sunk in, Blyth manager Brian Slane spoke of 'coming back from the dead' (not something you should try at home), and everyone toasted Terry Johnson who had only joined the club from Brentford at the start of the season because he was home-sick for his native north-east. The Blyth bandwagon was derailed by Wrexham in the next round but their Cup run did not go unrewarded. The squad, manager and coach were each given £350 worth of bedroom furniture by a local manufacturer. The *Blyth News Post* enthused: 'They can select from three types of bedroom unit – comprising of two wardrobes and a dressing table.' The FA Cup only gets dusty anyway...

'The ball came back to me off the post and I just put it in. It's just magic. I'm over the moon.'

Steve Carney's novel appraisal of his feelings

67

Halifax Town 1
Manchester City 0

5 January 1980

'It won't be the end of the world if we lose, but it will be close to that.'

Manchester City manager Malcolm Allison before the game

To Halifax, a good Cup run was a first-round replay. So when they put out Scarborough and Walsall to reach the third round in 1980, some West Yorkshire folk probably had to be treated for shock. The next visitors to The Shay were Manchester City, at the time seventh from the foot of the First Division, a healthy position compared to Halifax's mid-table berth in Division Four. But for years City had been great under-achievers. The previous season, they had been knocked out at Third Division Shrewsbury and had sought to remedy the situation by making Steve Daley Britain's costliest player. Despite all the spending, the Maine Road faithful remained far from impressed.

Whatever City's deficiencies, Halifax reckoned they needed all the help they could get. Accordingly, manager George Kirby enlisted the services of Romark, the hypnotist who, four years earlier, had put a curse on Malcolm Allison, then in charge of Crystal Palace. The curse worked then and was to do so again now. As Allison discovered to his cost, hypnotists make dangerous enemies.

The Halifax groundstaff were at work before daylight on match-day, draining away surface water, but it was still a mud-heap by kick-off. City, whose back four contained three teenagers, had an early scare when Mick Kennedy's long throw fell for Paul Hendrie. But Town's £5,000 signing from Bristol Rovers sent a six-yard volley way off target. Then an inswinging corner from Stafford, who had been released by City as a schoolboy, deceived Joe Corrigan and hit the far post.

Anxious to ensure there was no repeat of Shrewsbury, City pulled themselves together and Town's 19-year-old keeper John Kilner made splendid saves to thwart first Bobby Shinton and then Michael Robinson. Marshalled by their young captain Dave Evans, who had once been selected by Aston Villa to mark Johann Cruyff in a UEFA Cup tie, Halifax held firm although they should have been punished midway through the second half when Shinton shot straight at Kilner's midriff from three yards. With 15 minutes to go and the game seemingly heading for a replay, Stafford crossed from the left, Smith produced a deft touch given the conditions and Hendrie coolly shot under Corrigan. Halifax were in dreamland.

City tried hard to summon up a reply and in the dying seconds, Daley nearly repaid a crumb if not a slice of his transfer fee with a 25-yard drive which flew just wide. But at the final whistle, the singing and cheering came from the Halifax fans. The only cry from the City ~· 'Allison out!' For some reason, Arthur Cox has never been subjected to an equivalent chant...

The unexpected triumph certainly captured the imagination of the success-starved locals. Halifax reported a rush on scarves, hats and even the club record. 'People keep popping in,' said the commercial manager excitedly. 'We are going to have to order more rosettes.'

Like two.

68

Harlow Town 1
Leicester City 0

8 January 1980

*W*hen Gary Lineker sits down with a mug of Horlicks to reminisce about the most memorable games of his glittering career, he will no doubt recall great occasions at Goodison Park, White Hart Lane and the Nou Camp Stadium, Barcelona. One venue he may choose to forget is the Sportcentre, Harlow. For it was there in 1980 that a young Lineker suffered probably the most embarrassing result of his entire career as Second Division Leicester were knocked out of the FA Cup by a ramshackle crew called Harlow Town.

Season 1979-80 was Harlow's centenary. They had never even progressed to the first round proper before. They couldn't hold down a place in the top half of the Isthmian League. When it came to the leading lights of non-League football, Harlow were definitely on the 'dimmer' switch. Yet it was as if fate had decreed that all those barren years should be wiped away at a stroke with a glorious triumph to mark the 100 years' celebrations. They began cautiously with a narrow victory over Leytonstone-Ilford in the first round. Then Third Division Southend were beaten after a replay to set up a third-round trip to Filbert Street.

That was where the fairytale should have ended but promotion-chasing Leicester allowed Neil Prosser to snatch an 89th-minute equaliser and a second meeting became necessary, at Harlow. It was a scrappy game to set before a record crowd. Leicester played too many long, diagonal crosses which failed to trouble a defence in which Tony Gough was outstanding. When Leicester's target men, Martin Henderson and Alan Young, did manage to get in headers, they lacked either power or accuracy and sometimes both. As for young Lineker, he was so anonymous he didn't even warrant a mention in accounts of the game.

Harlow were the more inventive side with Micky Mann and Prosser repeatedly stretching the Leicester defence. In the early stages, a dangerous Mann free-kick flew across the goal and Peter Twigg twice went close to scoring, once with a fine shot from all of 35 yards. At the other end, Harlow keeper Paul Kitson saved well from John O'Neill but had a fortunate escape when Young headed tamely into his arms from six yards.

The decisive goal was suitably messy. Mann's 41st-minute free-kick fell to 25-year-old company accountant John Mackenzie. As Mackenzie tried to flick the ball on, it rebounded off Leicester defender Larry May. Mackenzie reacted first to send a left-foot shot past Mark Wallington. The ball crept no more than 18 inches over the line before Tommy Williams hacked it clear. Happily for Harlow, the referee was on the spot to award a goal.

Leicester looked more purposeful in the second half. Young twice shot wide from good positions and May's dipping long-range shot just cleared the bar. Harlow had their chances too and Dennis Rofe was forced to head off the line from Mackenzie with Wallington beaten.

As the completion of 90 minutes brought jubilant fans onto the pitch to toast their heroes, Harlow manager Ian Wolstenholme had every reason to be pleased with himself. 'We played far better than on Saturday,' he said. 'Some of Leicester's younger players appeared to show their nerves and we took full advantage. Tactically, it went just as I wanted. We cut off the supply from Eddie Kelly in midfield and in the end thoroughly deserved to go through.'

Few supply lines were cut the following week as hungover Harlow crashed 3-0 in the League at home to Hayes. But they regained their spirit for the fourth-round tie at Watford which they gallantly lost 4-3, Mackenzie scoring twice. That Cup run went down as Harlow Town's greatest achievement. The club folded in 1992.

Harlow Town: Kitson; Wickendon, Flack, Gough, Clarke, Adnams, Mann, Austin, Prosser, Twigg, Mackenzie.
Leicester City: Wallington; Williams, Rofe, Goodwin, May, O'Neill, Lineker, Henderson, Young, Kelly, Smith.
Referee: Mr A. Robinson (Waterlooville)
Attendance: 9,723

'It came from a free-kick move we play. Micky Mann swung the ball over well, I played the ball onto a defender, it came back and I hit it – with my wrong foot! I was so pleased to see the ball go over the line.'

Harlow scorer John Mackenzie

Harlow centre-half Vic Clarke (left) moves forward to threaten the Leicester goal.

162

69

11 December 1982

'I'd anticipated the situation from the moment their keeper kicked the ball. I must have run about 70 yards. I saw Mark look up and I knew the cross was coming. It was a wonderful cross. I didn't let it hit the ground – I just whacked it. It was the most pleasing goal I've ever scored but I couldn't believe we were 3-2 up. I remember asking Trevor Finnigan: "Did it happen?" He replied: "Just keep running for another five minutes and we're through to the next round."'

Weymouth's late match-winner Gerry Pearson

*I*t wasn't only Gerry Pearson who couldn't believe that Weymouth were winning. None of the Cardiff players could believe it either. For it was a match which the Third Division promotion-chasers had totally dominated in the first half. They had gone in two up and it could easily have been five or six. A Weymouth victory looked as unlikely as a John Jensen hat-trick. Yet a remarkable second-half transformation saw the Terras of Weymouth, third in the Alliance Premier League, score three times to silence the Ninian Park faithful. Singing in the valleys was at a premium that night.

It had all looked so different in the first half. Cardiff forced ten corners to Weymouth's none and, apart from an early Andy Dibble save to deny Trevor Finnigan, were always in command. Weymouth keeper Kieron Baker was by far the busiest man on the pitch. He made good stops from the Bennett brothers, Garry and Dave, but missed a long-range effort from John Lewis which struck the post. A goal had to come and it duly arrived on the half-hour. Phil Dwyer headed a free-kick back into the danger zone where Roger Gibbins nodded past Baker. Six minutes later, Cardiff were two up. Dave Bennett released Jeff Hemmerman in acres of room and the latter scored easily from eight yards.

At this stage, the Weymouth defence had more holes than a piece of Emmenthal. But their manager Stuart Morgan, who, ironically, hailed from Swansea, could see a way back.

Three minutes into the second half, Weymouth forced their first corner. Moments later, Pearson sent a fierce shot flashing past the post. Then Paul Bodin scooped a Finnigan shot off the line. Suddenly, it was Cardiff's turn to be on the rack.

On 54 minutes, the comeback began. Brian Benjafield's cross was headed over Dibble at the far post by Anniello Iannone whose main claim to fame until then was that his was a great name for 'Hangman'.

Jolted into action, Cardiff resumed the offensive. Paul Morrell cleared Hemmerman's header off the line and Baker reacted smartly to foil Gibbins. But in the 78th minute, Weymouth were level. Dwyer was caught in possession by Iannone, allowing Finnigan to run on to the loose ball and score.

With five minutes remaining, Weymouth might have been expected to settle for a replay but slipshod City presented them with a chance for greater glory. Dibble's weak goal-kick only travelled as far as Weymouth winger Mark Baber. Looking up for support, he saw Pearson haring into the middle. The cross was precise and so was the finish. Cardiff were out of the Cup and Weymouth were into the third round.

For the Terras' physio Bob Lucas, it brought back happy memories. He had been a member of the Weymouth team which came from 2-0 down to win 3-2 at Aldershot back in 1949.

70

AFC Bournemouth 2
Manchester United 0

7 January 1984

*C*up holders Manchester United came to Bournemouth second in
*Division One with a solitary away defeat all season. By
contrast, Bournemouth were fourth from the foot of Division Three
with just five home wins. The previous Monday, United had drawn
at Anfield while Bournemouth lost at bottom-of-the-table Port Vale.
An upset in this third-round Cup tie seemed inconceivable. But, as
someone once said, football is a funny old game.*

Bournemouth manager Harry Redknapp had watched a video of
United's recent League Cup defeat against Third Division Oxford and
had noticed 'a chink in their armour. Some of them do not perform
when they are closed down, and that was our main priority.' So
Bournemouth, rather like their predecessors of 1957, produced some
uncompromising tackles to unnerve the opposition. Bournemouth
centre-half Roger Brown said that he could see after just five minutes
that at least half of the United side were 'visibly frightened'.

Whether Bournemouth would have been able to streamroller a full-
strength United defence is open to question. But both Gordon

McQueen and Kevin Moran were out injured and 19-year-old debutant Graeme Hogg was a less resilient replacement. In fairness to Hogg, the jitters spread throughout the whole defence. Arthur Albiston was embarrassed early on while keeper Gary Bailey made a hash of an innocuous cross from Thompson. The first clear chance of the match fell to Bournemouth winger Milton Graham, a player who had polished his game in New Zealand the previous summer. But his left-foot drive from eight yards was deflected for a corner. United forced plenty of corners of their own in the opening half but their best effort was a free-kick by Dutchman Arnold Muhren which swerved just over the bar.

With Ron Atkinson having to reorganise the defence yet again – substitute Lou Macari coming on in the unaccustomed role of full-back – it was all they could do to keep Bournemouth at bay. United's resistance finally crumbled on the hour. Bailey dropped Sulley's corner and Milton Graham bundled the ball in from close range. Two minutes later, United fell to another sucker punch. La Ronde's free-kick landed at the feet of Bryan Robson, but even the great were fallible at Dean Court that afternoon. Robson failed to clear, enabling Thompson, a £16,000 signing from Salisbury, to dispossess him and score with a firm right-foot shot.

United never recovered from the double blow. Thus in the space of a month, they had bowed out of the two major domestic Cup competitions to Third Division opposition. At the end, George Best, working as a radio commentator, announced that he would have been 'embarrassed to pick up my week's wages', had he performed like some of the United players.

The following season, United were again drawn against Bournemouth in the third round. This time there were no mistakes, United cruising to a 3-0 win en route to winning the trophy itself. Normal service had been resumed.

'Defeat at Bournemouth was a horrible experience. Funnily enough, we beat Barcelona not long after in the Cup Winners' Cup and I told Maradona he could think himself lucky he hadn't been playing Bournemouth.'

Ron Atkinson

Milton Graham (dark strip, on floor) punishes Gary Bailey's blunder to put Bournemouth into a shock lead.

71

Preston North End 1
Telford United 4

8 December 1984

*N*o non-League team was more feared in the early 1980s than
Telford United. By the time they faced once-proud Preston in
the second round in 1984, they had won five of their seven encounters
with League teams over their previous two years, even though only
two of those ties had been at home. Wigan, Stockport, Northampton,
Rochdale and Lincoln had all bitten the dust. So a trip to Deepdale to
take on a Preston defence with a reputation for generosity
unsurpassed by the Lord's Taverners caused little loss of sleep in
Shropshire. The Preston faithful still pined for the days of Tom
Finney. In truth, even Albert Finney might have got a game in a side
which, with 45 goals conceded in 18 Third Division fixtures, boasted
the worst defensive record in the entire Football League.

The Alliance team always looked like gaining a famous victory but
even they were surprised at the ease with which it was accomplished.
The two chief destroyers were midfielder Paul Mayman, who
launched many of the assaults on the home goal, and striker Colin
Williams, only passed fit to play at the eleventh hour. Williams gave
an early taste of what was to come with a header which Peter
Litchfield had to turn over the bar but Telford's lead was only
delayed for a few minutes. Mayman won a corner on the right and
helped John Alcock to work a short flag-kick routine. When Alcock's
cross came over, Williams glanced it on for left-back Turner to steal in
and stab past Litchfield from six yards.

Such was Telford's superiority that it was something of a shock when
the League side drew level on 35 minutes, Hunter firing home after
McAteer's shot had struck the inside of a post. Telford stepped up
another gear at the start of the second half. Ken McKenna broke down

the right and unleashed a ground shot. Litchfield dived too early and could only help the ball into the net. Three minutes later, it was 3-1, albeit somewhat fortuitously. Williams ran through the heart of what passed as the Preston defence and shot for goal. It got there, but by the scenic route. For the shot struck a defender and rebounded onto Williams' knee from whence it looped into the net just inside the post. Williams completed the rout by rounding the exposed Litchfield and slotting home the fourth. He could have had two more, heading Alcock's cross over the top and then missing the target with just Litchfield to beat.

If it was any consolation to Preston, it was that they had lost to a very good non-League side, one which went on to account for Bradford City and Darlington before going down 3-0 at Everton in the fifth round. But that would have mattered little to the long-suffering North End fans drowning their sorrows in the pubs of Preston that Saturday night.

Preston North End: Litchfield; M.Jones, McAteer, D.Jones, Twentyman, Clark, McGee, Gray, Johnson, Naughton, Houston (Hunter).
Telford United: Charlton; Lewis, Turner, Mayman, Eaton, Hancock, Joseph, Williams, McKenna, Hogan, Alcock.
Referee: Mr P. Tyldesley (Stockport)
Attendance: 6,134

'If you'd gone to the ground not knowing who the teams were, you'd never have guessed we were the non-League side. They were the ones who looked nervous, and I fancied us after ten minutes. Even the Preston supporters were cheering us towards the end.'

Telford manager Stan Storton

72

York City 1
Arsenal 0

26 January 1985

'It was going to be a goalless draw all the way. It was that sort of match.'

Arsenal boss Don Howe

*L*ike Queens Park Rangers, who lost at Doncaster three weeks earlier, Arsenal travelled north with a well-rehearsed offside trap and the intention of avoiding defeat at all costs. Perhaps it was the news that the Bootham Crescent pitch would be bone-hard and liberally sprinkled with snow that determined their caution but the £4.5 million Arsenal team were taking no chances against a York squad assembled for just £19,000. Of that, £15,000 had been spent on bringing striker Keith Houchen from Orient.

Newly promoted from the Fourth Division, York had been on a strict diet of Cup glory since their famous victory over Spurs in 1955 although they had earned a creditable draw at Highbury in 1975 before losing the replay. Now ten years on, they had accounted for Blue Star from the Wearside League, Hartlepool United and Walsall without conceding a goal but would surely be severely tested by an Arsenal side fresh from a 7-2 demolition of Hereford in a third-round replay.

With Stewart Robson, Steve Williams and Brian Talbot stifling the midfield with biting tackles, the match was not exactly one for the connoisseur. Arsenal's one flair player, Charlie Nicholas. was so ineffective on the surface that he was eventually substituted. It was an indictment of his fellow forwards that Arsenal's best chance was created by a buccaneering run down the wing from full-back Kenny Sansom. His cross appeared destined for Paul Mariner, only to be diverted to safety at the last minute by a flick of Hay's head.

York were no better. For 89 minutes, they mustered nothing more than two half chances. Ford missed one by the proverbial mile while Keith Walwyn sent the other hurtling out of the ground in the direction of Harrogate.

The referee was looking at his watch. There were just seconds remaining. Many of the crowd had drifted off to the warmth of their homes. Arsenal seemed to have got the replay they had come for. York were looking forward to a nice pay-day at Highbury. The BBC were scratching their heads, wondering how they could possibly stretch the action to five minutes on Match of the Day that night. Then Walwyn headed the ball forward for the umpteenth time. It was a harmless enough situation but he loped after it and managed to squeeze the ball out to Butler on the right. In a rare display of vision, Butler immediately whipped over the cross. It was aimed towards a space where Houchen might arrive but he never got there. En route, in an off-the-ball clash, he was needlessly impeded by Williams. The referee pointed to the spot. As the 90th minute registered, Houchen stepped up, sent John Lukic to the right and coolly slotted the ball low into the opposite corner.

Few outside Finsbury Park shed any tears for Arsenal. They were given a reminder of what might have been in the next round when York, after holding Liverpool at Bootham Crescent, crashed 7-0 at Anfield. At least Keith Houchen enjoyed some success, scoring at Wembley two years later to help Coventry lift the Cup at the expense of Arsenal's great North London rivals Tottenham.

York City: Astbury; Senior, Sbragia, McPhail, Hay, Ford, Houchen, Haselgrave, Pearce, Walwyn, Butler.
Arsenal: Lukic; Anderson, O'Leary, Caton, Sansom, Talbot, Williams, Robson, Mariner, Woodcock, Nicholas (Allinson).
Referee: Mr D. Shaw (Sandbach)
Attendance: 10,840

73

Birmingham City 1
Altrincham 2

14 January 1986

*L*ike Telford, Altrincham were seasoned giant-killers. They had
seen off no fewer than 11 League sides over the previous 20 years
but their biggest scalp was that of First Division Birmingham in a
third-round tie in 1986.

Birmingham were a First Division side in name only – and even then,
only temporarily. Anchored near the foot of the table, they hadn't
won in 17 games and were £2.25 million in the red. There was no
money for manager Ron Saunders to enter the transfer market and
those players who were there moaned about the lack of heating in the
dressing-rooms. Such was the club's plight that a 70-year-old
pensioner was responsible for the entire maintenance of St Andrew's.
In the circumstances, it was perhaps not too surprising that a
Birmingham season-ticket holder was quoted as saying that 99 per
cent of Blues' fans expected them to lose to Altrincham.

For once, the Birmingham fans' expectations were realised. By
adopting the elementary practice of keeping the ball on the ground,
the Gola League team coped with the gale-force conditions far better
than their supposedly superior opponents. *The Times* commented that
Birmingham's 'crude up and under style fell easy prey to a wind
which almost uprooted the stand flags from their moorings.'
Altrincham were particularly effective in the second half when they
were kicking into the teeth of the gale. As a result, former City keeper
Jeff Wealands was rarely troubled in the visitors' goal. Wealands,
who was working in insurance in Manchester, had been released by
Birmingham three years earlier when Saunders took over as manager.
He had a point to prove.

With fewer than 7,000 in the ground, St Andrew's was grimmer than usual that night. There was more atmosphere on the moon. For a fleeting, improbable moment, it appeared that the home support's fears were unfounded. On 62 minutes, lively winger Robert Hopkins put the Blues ahead. But it was soon back to reality. A free-kick from Davison swerved in the wind and as it dropped in the goalmouth, Ellis found space to jab home the equaliser. Then in the 74th minute came an appropriately comic winner. Hopkins, who 12 minutes earlier had been his side's possible saviour, found himself under pressure facing his own goal. England Under-21 goalkeeper David Seaman came out to intercept but Hopkins' intended back pass slid beyond him and into the unguarded net.

While Altrincham boss John King saluted his players, Ron Saunders lamented: 'This has been coming for two years...our prospects of staying in the First Division do not look bright.' He was right about that. Just over three months later, Birmingham were relegated. Their ability was put into perspective when Altrincham were comfortably beaten at Third Division York in the next round.

Birmingham City: Seaman; Ranson, Dicks, Hagan, Armstrong, Kuhl, Roberts, Wright, Kennedy, Platnauer, Hopkins.
Altrincham: Wealands; Gardner, Densmore, Johnson, Cuddy, Conning, Ellis, Davison, Reid, Chesters, Anderson.
Referee: Mr K. Hackett (Sheffield)
Attendance: 6,636

'We were worthy winners. I fancied our chances right from when the draw was made. They didn't really put us under any pressure whatsoever. From a personal point of view, it's a very sweet win. The problems I had with the manager here are well known.'

Altrincham's former Birmingham goalkeeper Jeff Wealands

74

Chorley 3
Wolverhampton Wanderers 0

24 November 1986

*I*t was the finest day in Chorley's 103-year history. The Northern Premier League outfit had never before knocked a Football League side out of the FA Cup but now they broke their duck in style, ousting one of the most famous names in the game, Wolverhampton Wanderers, a club which, six years previously, had been playing in Europe.

But this was not the Wolves of Cullis and Wright. It wasn't even the Wolves of Dougan and Richards. This was the Wolves that was in its fifth manager in two years. It was the Wolves that was sampling its first-ever taste of life in the Fourth Division; a club which had fallen on hard times, one that wanted 10p – if not for a cup of tea, then for a centre-forward. Just as this was to be Chorley's moment of glory, it was also to mark the lowest point in Wolves' own 109-year history.

Chorley were no great shakes themselves and were struggling in their own modest League. But they were more than a match for Wolves. Chorley's own little ground was not big enough to cope with the expected Wolves' following so the first match was switched to neutral Burnden Park, Bolton. It ended 1-1. So did the second meeting at Molineux, thanks in no small part to Chorley's inspired keeper Ian Senior. It was back to Bolton for the third game, a match in which, according to the *Wolverhampton Express & Star*, Chorley 'made Wolves look like a pub team.' Such was the slur that Dog and Ferret Reserves were thought to be contemplating legal action.

Chorley had come from behind in the first two encounters but needed no such courage here. After 17 minutes, former Stafford Rangers forward Phil Marsden waited for a team-mate to come back from an offside position before releasing Charlie Cooper with a beautifully-angled through ball. Cooper ran onto it, rounded keeper Vince Bartram and slotted into the empty net. Wolves managed only two shots in the whole of the first half, both long-range efforts from Jon Purdie. He put the first onto the roof of the stand and sliced the second yards wide.

On 52 minutes, Chorley made it two. Post office clerk Mark Edwards wrestled his way past Peter Zelem and coolly lobbed Bartram. Twenty minutes later, Steve Phillips teed up a simple third for Cooper as Wolves disintegrated completely. As *The Times* put it, they were 'now an anonymous, mediocre Fourth Division side.'

As he went on a lap of honour at the end of the game to celebrate his side's first appearance in the second round, Chorley keeper Senior had the cleanest knees in Bolton. The *Express & Star* did not mince words. 'You would think things can get no worse. But in their current plight, Graham Turner's side can be expected to give it a good try.'

In fact, things got better rather than worse. In the middle of the three matches with Chorley, Turner, who had only been manager at Molineux for a month, signed unknown striker Steve Bull on the cheap from West Brom. Bull's goals helped Wolves reach the Fourth Division play-offs that season. And, although it took another eight years and a number of clubs, Jon Purdie finally found his shooting boots...as Birmingham City would discover to their cost.

Chorley: Senior; Scott, Hughes, Webster (Lloyd), Roberts, Cooper, Phillips, Marsden, Edwards (Clarke), Moss, Nichol.
Wolverhampton Wanderers: Bartram; Stoutt, Barnes, Zelem, Forman, Robertson, Edwards, Holmes, Mutch, K. Lockhart (D. Lockhart), Purdie.
Referee: Mr R. Bridges
Attendance: 5,421

'Chorley brushed us aside. It was men against boys. It's not even as if we were unfortunate. We had three cracks at them, yet finished well beaten. They had more conviction and more character. Alistair

175

Robertson pulled a thigh muscle in the first ten minutes and was still our best player. That says a lot.'

Wolves's honest manager Graham Turner

75

Port Vale 2
Tottenham Hotspur 1

30 January 1988

'This cold, damp dressing-room is our secret weapon for Spurs – not forgetting their lukewarm pot of tea at half-time.'

Port Vale defender Phil Sproson welcoming Tottenham to the Potteries

Terry Venables knew Spurs would be in for a rough ride. That's why he dropped Ossie Ardiles for this fourth-round tie, reasoning that the little Argentinian's silky skills would be buried alive on the mud-heap that went under the deceptively sylvan name of Vale Park. Venables knew that Spurs would have to scrap for everything against a Vale side which was sure to play above its position of 18th in the Third Division. The trouble was, the message didn't seem to get through to his players.

Where were Tottenham's stars? Clive Allen was anonymous, Terry Fenwick was a model of uncertainty and Chris Waddle confirmed the belief that he hibernates in winter. And all of this against a team which had struggled to overcome Macclesfield in the previous round and were priced at 1,000-1 for the Cup. Few of Vale's own supporters thought those odds to be over-generous.

Right from the start, it was apparent that Tottenham's attitude was wrong. In the opening exchanges, Vale's combative captain Bob Hazell was heard to remark to his team-mates: 'They don't fancy it…' He was right. Spurs didn't like it up 'em!

True, Waddle did have the opportunity to soothe the visiting nerves but once he had stabbed harmlessly wide of Mark Grew's goal, the pressure was all at the other end. The intimidating figure of Neil Ruddock, who makes Tommy Smith look anorexic, was hurried into two wild back passes, both of which went for corners, one needing a diving save from Tony Parks. Vale were content to pump long balls down the middle and hope for the best. They didn't have long to wait. On 12 minutes, Phil Sproson (whose uncle Roy played a record 761 games for the club between 1950 and 1972) swept a pass forward to Ray Walker, a £12,000 snip from Aston Villa. Walker responded by unleashing a superb 25-yard drive which dipped, swerved and utterly bamboozled Parks. The Vale fans and the Match of the Day producer rejoiced in unison.

If Parks deserved some sympathy over the first goal, he merited none for the second 12 minutes later. When Walker flighted a free-kick into the box, Parks made a mess of his punch. In the melee, Darren Beckford had a shot blocked before Sproson lashed the loose ball high into the net.

Whatever its temperature, the half-time cuppa did little to refresh Spurs although Ruddock managed to pull one back after 62 minutes with a typically powerful header from Waddle's free-kick. Ruddock, at least, began to roll his sleeves up in the last half-hour, atoning for his earlier clumsiness. However his colleagues failed to respond to his battle cry and, despite the customary late flourish from teams anxious to avoid embarrassing Sunday morning headlines, Spurs never really looked like coming up with an equaliser.

Vale's goalscoring heroes were none too charitable in their post-match summing-up. Sproson derided Spurs as being 'just like West Ham used to be – all fancy flicks and sweet sherry.' Walker added: 'It was drummed into us that they wouldn't have much ammunition on a pitch where they couldn't play their one-twos. It took them an hour to get adjusted.'

Port Vale: Grew; Steggles, Hazell, Sproson, Hughes, Ford, Walker, Earle, Beckford (Finney), Cole, Riley.
Tottenham Hotspur: Parks; Hughton (Howells), Fairclough, Ruddock, Thomas, P. Allen, Fenwick, Waddle, Mabbutt, C. Allen, Moran.
Referee: Mr D. Scott (Burnley)
Attendance: 20,045

76

Middlesbrough 1
Grimsby Town 2

7 January 1989

'The FA Cup can be very romantic – but not for us.'
Middlesbrough manager Bruce Rioch

*G*rimsby Town's first-ever appearance in the FA Cup was an occasion to remember. Back in 1882, they were drawn at home to the mighty Glasgow club Queen's Park but when the Scots withdrew from the competition, Town received a bye into the second round where they entertained less glamorous opponents in Phoenix Bessemer, a Rotherham works side. Grimsby proceeded to go down 9-1. Perhaps it was as well that Queen's Park had pulled out...

The next 107 years produced nothing more than two losing semi-finals for the Mariners (in 1936 and 1939), after which they failed to progress beyond the fourth round again until 1982. By the start of 1989, they were struggling at the wrong end of the Fourth Division. So despite early round victories over Wolves and Rotherham, respective leaders of the Third and Fourth Divisions, few of the 2,000 Grimsby fans who journeyed to Ayresome Park could have been too optimistic about the chances of success against a Middlesbrough side acquitting itself well in the First Division.

One cause for hope was that Middlesbrough boasted an even more miserable Cup record than Grimsby, never having even reached the semi-finals. Nevertheless, they were firm favourites for this third-round clash, particularly since they were eager to atone for a Littlewoods Cup dismissal by another Fourth Division team, Tranmere Rovers.

But cometh the hour, cometh the man. Marc North had been an irregular member of the Grimsby team over the previous 18 months and had to settle for a place on the substitutes' bench at Ayresome Park. His eventual entry was to turn the match in the most dramatic fashion.

Grimsby comfortably held their own for the first 40 minutes, their only scare coming in the 20th minute when Paul Reece had to move swiftly to thwart Peter Davenport. Five minutes later, Shaun Cunnington fastened on to a through ball from John McDermott but, after running nearly half the length of the pitch, was foiled by Steve Pears in the home goal. It seemed that Grimsby would go in on level terms until that arch goal-poacher Bernie Slaven struck on 40 minutes. Gary Hamilton crossed from the left, Stuart Ripley helped it on and there was Slaven waiting to pounce.

The second period saw Grimsby begin to cause the much-vaunted central pairing of Tony Mowbray and new England international Gary Pallister considerable discomfort. On 54 minutes, Pears saved well from Richard O'Kelly and 11 minutes later, Keith Alexander fired over from a promising position. Sensing a need for greater purpose in front of goal, manager Alan Buckley decided to replace O'Kelly with North in the 70th minute. The substitution took place during a break for a Grimsby throw-in. Richard Jobling's throw found Alexander who beat Pallister and passed to North inside the box. The substitute turned sharply and drove past Pears to score with his first touch of the ball.

Buckley said afterwards: 'I wanted to put Marc on when we were in an attacking position and it paid off immediately.'

'Boro came storming back and Pallister headed against the bar with Reece beaten. Then with three minutes remaining, Jobling and Alexander combined once more. The latter's cross eluded Pears and North dived between two defenders to head home from six yards to round off a fairytale afternoon.

North later revealed: 'The gaffer told me at half-time that I'd go on if we were still losing. I had not been playing well in recent matches and the fans were impatient with me. So this was a great day for me.' The defeat had a disastrous effect on Middlesbrough's season and they found themselves sucked into the relegation struggle. Come May, they learned that they would be playing Second Division football the following term. Grimsby went on to beat Reading in the fourth round before bowing out 3-1 at Wimbledon in the fifth where the sight of ranks of Grimsby supporters waving inflatable haddocks launched a thousand crazes. Soon there were inflatable bananas and hammers on the terraces to go with the inflated wages on the pitch.

Middlesbrough: Pears; Burke, Cooper, Mowbray, Hamilton, Pallister, Slaven (Mohan), Brennan, Glover, Davenport, Ripley.
Grimsby Town: Reece; McDermott, Agnew, Tillson, Lever, Cunnington, Jobling, Saunders, O'Kelly (North), Cockerill, Alexander.
Referee: Mr A. Seville (Birmingham)
Attendance: 19,190

77

Sutton United 2
Coventry City 1

7 January 1989

*T*he history of Coventry City is littered with Cup disasters. Back in 1897, when they were known as Singers FC, they lost 1-0 in the first preliminary round to the village amateurs of Wrockwardine

Wood. In 1925, they went out by a similar score in the first round at Worksop, most of whose team had spent the morning of the match working down a local coalmine. When the Midland Leaguers scored, the Worksop chairman invaded the pitch! Another Midland League side, Scunthorpe, put them out in 1935 and then there was King's Lynn in 1961. By 1970 when Monty Python posed the question, 'In which year did Coventry City win the FA Cup?', everyone except Karl Marx knew that it was a trick question. Coventry City had never won the FA Cup. They eventually remedied that situation in 1987 but, as if not wishing to disappoint their followers, reserved their greatest humiliation of all for two years later.

Gander Green Lane, Sutton, is not a venue to strike fear into the hearts of the opposition. It is no Den, no Anfield. Set in South London suburbia where tidy people own tidy houses with tidy lawns, in 1989 it was home to a club which had its own wine committee and was managed by a former English teacher with a penchant for quoting Shakespeare, Kipling and the Venerable Bead in his programme notes. Barrie Williams would rather have shot himself than be 'sick as a parrot'. His Vauxhall Conference team included two assistant bank managers, two insurance executives and a commodity broker.

Coventry were fifth in the First Division and paraded seven of their Cup-winning side. It seemed no contest. But after watching Coventry three times, the perceptive Williams had detected a weakness at set pieces and spent most of the morning of the match practising corners with his players in a public park behind the ground. Nothing went right. Corners were too short or too long, leaving Williams cursing in language which owed more to the factory floor than the Bard. Yet, as if by magic, a few hours later, the corners worked to perfection as Sutton United created the biggest upset since Wimbledon won at Burnley.

On 41 minutes, Mickey Stephens' corner was flicked on by Golley for Tony Rains, playing his 613th game for the club, to head home at the far post. David Phillips levelled for Coventry seven minutes after the break before another Stephens corner brought the winner in the 58th minute. This time Stephens played it short to Dawson whose

One of the great Cup sensations. Matthew Hanlan (11) knocks Sutton's winner past the lunge of Coventry's Steve Ogrizovic.

penetrating cross from the right found 22-year-old bricklayer Matthew Hanlan at the head of a queue of Sutton players waiting to knock the ball past Steve Ogrizovic.

Sutton then played the best football of the match. McKinnon (twice) and Dennis had chances to increase the lead and a flowing four-man move finished with Stephens firing narrowly wide. It was only in the anxious last ten minutes that Sutton were forced to defend. At the finish, the 2,500 Coventry supporters sportingly remained in their places to applaud the Sutton team. *The Times* wrote: 'The most remarkable FA Cup result for 14 years was a triumph for skill, tactical awareness and intelligent planning, qualities that have been going increasingly out of fashion in many areas of the game.' Barrie Williams would have liked that. As for Coventry, 12 months later, before setting out on their next Cup campaign, manager John Sillett predicted that the 'Sutton experience' had done his players good. He was speaking from the County Ground, Northampton, home of Third Division strugglers Northampton Town. Coventry lost 1-0.

Sutton lost 8-0 at Norwich in the fourth round.

Sutton United: Roffey; Jones, Rains, Golley, Pratt, Rogers, Stephens, Dawson, Dennis, McKinnon, Hanlan.
Coventry City: Ogrizovic; Borrows, Phillips, Sedgley, Kilcline, Peake, Bennett, Speedie, Regis (Houchen), McGrath, Smith.
Referee: Mr A. Buksh (Dollis Hill)
Attendance: 8,000

'While Coventry's players were away from their families most of the week, we've been doing our jobs and leading normal lives. We didn't feel any nerves, because we had nothing to lose. Coventry weren't very different from the teams we play every week in the Conference. We had more time on the ball than we usually get and it wasn't as hard physically as in our league. We've proved that professional sides aren't superstars – they're humans and can be beaten.'

Sutton captain Tony Rains

 78

Whitley Bay 2
Preston North End 0

9 December 1989

'I was surprised how poor Preston were. Maybe they were undone by their plastic pitch at home which means they play a short-passing game. That suited us.'

Whitley Bay manager Barry Graham

*F*or the best part of a century, Whitley Bay were the unknown team of Tyneside. Only eight miles away from St James's Park, they might as well have been on another planet. Jackie Milburn was someone whose column they read in the News of the World.

Whitley Bay first entered the FA Cup in 1908, yet it was not until 1989 when, as members of the Northern Premier League, they finally made the first round proper. Having waited so long for a taste of glory, they made an immediate impact, winning 1-0 at Scarborough to earn a plum home tie with Preston. Although North End were floundering in the lower half of the Third Division, they were expected to prove far too strong for a team which was only in the First Division (not the Premier) of their League. Manager John McGrath, the former Newcastle defender, stated: 'If we don't win, there is something sadly wrong.' Nevertheless, Preston were understandably wary of any repeat of the Telford debacle of five years earlier.

Epitomising the enthusiasm at that level, Whitley Bay's schoolteacher manager Barry Graham made an 18-hour round trip to spy on Preston at Cardiff. He returned to the north-east convinced that he had spotted a few weaknesses. He was proved to be correct.

With Whitley Bay's tiny ground filled to capacity and the Match of the Day cameras present to capture the occasion, Preston soon began to look decidedly uneasy. In midfield, Whitley Bay's Paul Walker completely overshadowed Ian Bogie who, in his Newcastle United days, was once hailed as the new Gazza. He was last heard of playing for Leyton Orient. With no room to manoeuvre on the tight pitch and their close-passing tactics falling prey to the bog-like conditions, it was really no surprise when Preston fell behind in the 32nd minute. A fierce drive by Kevin Todd (who had played with Kevin Keegan at Newcastle) was only half cleared and former Darlington man Peter Robinson was on hand to net the rebound. Whitley Bay never looked back. Apart from a couple of first-half saves, Brian Dickson in the home goal was a virtual spectator. Todd sealed it on the hour, producing a fine drive to finish off a great 60-yard run from Tony Dawson. Such was the ineptitude of the opposition that the non-Leaguers were confident enough to order the statutory champagne well before the final whistle. There was never any danger of it having to be put on ice

Whitley Bay's miserly reward was a third-round trip to Rochdale where they lost 1-0. It was back to Newcastle Brown.

79

West Bromwich Albion 2
Woking 4

5 January 1991

*T*owards the end of 1990, Woking manager Geoff Chapple *scratched his head after seeing his side slump to a 4-2 Isthmian League defeat at the hands of Kingstonian. 'I don't know what's wong with Tim,' he puzzled. 'But he's just not the player we know. He's been having an indifferent season but you've got to pick him as first choice because you know what he can do.'*

The 'Tim' in question was Tim Buzaglo, football enigma and sometime cricketer for Gibraltar. Two months later, Buzaglo suggested that predictions of his demise were somewhat premature with a stunning hat-trick to sink Second Division West Brom in a remarkable third-round tie at The Hawthorns.

Woking had never previously beaten a League team and, for the first half, did not look like doing so this time either. The Woking game plan was to expose West Brom's slow defenders but the tactic was rendered redundant as the Woking players seemed to freeze on the big occasion. It was 16 minutes before they managed a shot at goal and it came as no surprise when Albion took the lead in the 35th minute, Colin West heading in a Craig Shakespeare corner.

Woking manager Geoff Chapple (left) and hat-trick hero Tim Buzaglo (centre) greet the news of a fourth round tie with Everton.

The goal appeared to jolt Woking into action although there was still no indication of what was to come. Then Buzaglo took centre stage, his game transformed in a manner previously seen only with Popeye under the effects of spinach. On 59 minutes, he ran at central defenders Strodder and Roberts, played a one-two with Brown and calmly stroked the return past Rees with his left foot. Six minutes later, Tim Read's long goal kick was flicked on by Brown to send Buzaglo haring through again. Rees raced out but his sliding challenge merely lobbed the ball into the air, leaving Buzaglo to head in the rebound. The hat-trick was completed in the 72nd minute. Pratt and Biggins exchanged passes near the right touchline and when Cowler helped on Biggins' cross, the unmarked Buzaglo brought it down and hammered a vicious left-foot drive into the net. Two minutes from time, Shane Wye crossed for substitute Worsfold to mark his first touch by sending a diving header past Rees. When Darren Bradley pulled one back in the last minute, his goal was booed by by the West Brom supporters!

At full-time, the West Brom fans ran over to the 4,000-strong Woking contingent and applauded them before calling for their own board and manager to resign. The Albion faithful then hoisted Buzaglo onto their shoulders for a lap of honour. Even Lee Dixon has yet to achieve such popularity with opposing fans as to be chaired off by them. Three days later, Brian Talbot was sacked as West Brom manager, another casualty of giant-killing. Drawn at home to Everton in the fourth round, Woking switched the tie to Goodison Park where they gave a magnificent account of themselves before being nudged out 1-0.

West Bromwich Albion: Rees; Bradley, Strodder, Roberts, Harbey (Palmer), Ford, Robson, McNally, Shakespeare, West, Bannister.
Woking: Read; Mitchell, Pratt, Cowler, Baron, S.Wye, Brown, L.Wye, Biggins, Buzaglo, Franks (Worsfold).
Referee: Mr R. Hamer (Bristol)
Attendance: 15,100

'When West Brom scored, I think our boys felt they might as well start making a game of it then. Buzaglo is a very laid back man who just decides to do these things now and again.'

Woking manager Geoff Chapple

80

Wrexham 2
Arsenal 1

4 January 1992

It was a shot in a million. Throughout his long career, Welsh international Mickey Thomas had never hit one quite like it. His Wrexham team-mates could hardly believe it. They said it was the first time all season he had even so much as hit the target from a similar position, either in training or competition. It was Arsenal's misfortune to be on the receiving end.

Wrexham's Steve Watkin is hugged by delirious team-mates after scoring the decisive goal against Arsenal.

Thomas was 37 when he ran out onto the Racecourse Ground in an unlikely bid to help Wrexham, bottom of the Football League the previous season, knock out reigning champions Arsenal. The gulf between the two clubs could not have been greater. Thomas himself admitted before the match that Arsenal were 'on a different planet in footballing terms.'

Thomas had played against Arsenal, for Manchester United, in the 1979 final. United lost that day. Revenge was to be sweet for the little Welshman.

Arsenal dominated the first half and, but for Vince O'Keefe in the Wrexham goal, would have gone in with a commanding lead. In the second minute, Phillips cleared off the line from Alan Smith and three minutes later, Jimmy Carter shot wide from 12 yards with the goal at his mercy. As it was, their only reward came two minutes before the interval. Paul Merson outpaced Mark Sertori on the left and pulled back for Smith to score easily.

The Gunners nearly increased their lead in the 62nd minute but Nigel Winterburn's drive struck the underside of the bar. Even so, with their notoriously mean defence, it still seemed probable that one goal would be sufficient to take Arsenal into the fourth round.

Then in two unbelievable minutes, Arsenal's world fell apart. It began in the 82nd minute when Wrexham were awarded a controversial free-kick 20 yards out, the referee deciding that David O'Leary had fouled 36-year-old Gordon Davies, the second of Wrexham's 'two old gits'. Thomas shaped to take the kick. The crowd behind the goal ducked. People in Llangollen hastily boarded up windows. But for once his aim was true. The ball flew as straight as an arrow into David Seaman's top right-hand corner. Wrexham were level.

The cheers were still ringing out when shell-shocked Arsenal conceded a throw-in down the Wrexham right. Andy Thackeray's throw was flicked on by Gareth Owen to Davies who turned and crossed. Tony Adams fumbled the clearance and 20-year-old Steve Watkin snaked a leg round the Arsenal captain to poke the ball past Seaman.

The result was so unexpected that Wrexham hadn't bothered to order any champagne. Instead celebrations were confined to a few beers in the players' lounge. Delighted Wrexham manager Brian Flynn claimed that if Thomas were ten years younger, he could sell him for £5 million. After the game, Seaman presented his goalkeeping gloves to Thomas's 11-year-old son. Thomas said: 'It was nice of him: he's a real professional. Or perhaps he doesn't want to wear them again...'

Thomas was soon to make headlines of a different kind when imprisoned for his part in a forged £10 note racket, an episode which earned him a new nickname, 'the Welsh tenner'.

'They're big stars and you can see on the television that when things don't go their way, they tend to get a bit rattled. I thought they were going to be a lot more professional when they were leading and tighten it up. They treated it as a training match. We've got a team of youngsters and two old men, and perhaps our desire to win was greater than theirs.'

Wrexham's Gordon Davies

81

Birmingham City 1
Kidderminster Harriers 2

8 January 1994

*B*efore the game, Birmingham manager Barry Fry predicted with typical honesty: 'If I was Kidderminster boss, I would really fancy my chances.' It was no idle prophecy. In his couple of months at the club, Fry had spent £1.27 million on nine new players but had yet to find a drawing, let alone a winning, formula. For their part, Kidderminster were top of the GM Vauxhall Conference and managed by lifelong Birmingham fan, Graham Allner. The previous season, Harriers had been struggling against relegation but chairman David Reynolds had refused to be panicked into sacking Allner, now in his 11th year with the club. In 108 years, Kidderminster had never beaten a League club but this time they had an ace in their pack in Jon Purdie, a former England schoolboy international with Tony Adams and David Rocastle at Arsenal. He had since moved on to Wolves

After Birmingham, Kidderminster went on to defeat Preston 1-0. Delwyn Humphries (second from left) celebrates his winner.

(where he was a member of the team which lost to Chorley), Oxford, Shrewsbury and Cambridge United before joining Kidderminster. He had only played in front of a big crowd once before – for Oxford at Old Trafford. 'I completely froze that day,' he said, 'and I was determined it wouldn't happen again.'

Still haunted by memories of Altrincham, the Blues' fans saw their side get off to a perfect start, Paul Harding converting a right-wing cross to put them ahead in the ninth minute. But as with most Birmingham leads, it couldn't last. On 28 minutes, Bancroft overlapped down the left and crossed to the far post where Cartwright scored with a downward header.

Birmingham pushed forward but Brindley and Weir stood firm at the back against a barrage of crosses from Ted McMinn and when they were beaten, Rose pulled off a string of fine saves. But with City looking by far the likelier to score, Purdie produced a moment of class in the 63rd minute to make one wonder what he was doing playing non-League football. Knowing that Purdie favoured his left foot, Birmingham's experienced central defender Chris Whyte allowed him to cut inside. Accepting the bait, Purdie promptly hit a right-foot drive from 25 yards which soared high into the net beyond Bennett's despairing dive. Later, Purdie admitted: 'You get in situations like that in every game, but rarely do they fly in like that. Usually they trickle wide or finish up in the stand.'

Their pride at stake, Birmingham roared back on to the attack. Hodson nodded Whyte's header off the line, Kenny Lowe's volley struck a post and Andy Saville had a goal ruled out for offside as Kidderminster rode their luck. Even the award of a penalty, after Lowe had been bundled over by Hodson, could not bring an equaliser. Saville's spot-kick beat Rose but bounced to safety off the top of the right-hand post. Along with the other 364 in an average year, it was not Birmingham City's day.

Birmingham City: Bennett; Hiley, Whyte, Dryden, Cooper, Parris, Lowe, Harding (Smith), McMinn, Donowa (Willis), Saville.
Kidderminster Harriers: Rose; Hodson, Brindley, Weir, Bancroft, Deakin, Grainger, Forsyth, Purdie, Cartwright, Humphreys.
Referee: Mr T. West
Attendance: 19,666

'We've let the club down. A lot of Birmingham fans will be degraded and humiliated. They will go into work and take a lot of stick. It will take a long time for them to get over it. Never mind that we had so many chances. All they will see is that we are out of the Cup.'

Birmingham City boss Barry Fry